Teacher's Manual

Book 1
Mathematical
Reasoning
through Verbal Analysis

SERIES TITLES
Mathematical Reasoning Book 1, Mathematical Reasoning Book 2

Warren Hill & Ronald Edwards

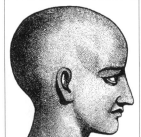

© 1988
CRITICAL THINKING BOOKS & SOFTWARE
www.CriticalThinking.com
P.O. Box 448 • Pacific Grove • CA 93950-0448
Phone 800-458-4849 • FAX 831-393-3277
ISBN 0-89455-359-3
Printed in the United States of America

ABOUT THE AUTHORS

WARREN H. HILL is a Professor of Mathematics at Westfield State College in Massachusetts. Dr. Hill holds doctorates in mathematics and psychology from Peabody College for Teachers. He earned a B.Ed. at Keene State College and an M.S.T. in mathematics from the University of New Hampshire. He has been at Westfield for twenty-one years where he teaches undergraduate and graduate courses in mathematics. In addition, Dr. Hill conducts seminars for undergraduate and graduate students that focus upon the application of analytic and critical thinking to problem-solving activities and the acquisition of number, spatial, and verbal concepts by children. Prior to his college teaching, he taught for several years at the high school level. Dr. Hill presents workshops and papers at state, national, and international conferences and serves as a consultant to school districts across the country. He is the author of many articles and books on mathematics and the application of thinking skills to a wide range of academic disciplines.

RONALD R. EDWARDS is a Professor of Mathematics at Westfield State College in Massachusetts. Dr. Edwards is a Phi Beta Kappa from Brown University where he received an A.B. degree in mathematics. He also earned an M.A.T. from Wesleyan University and a Ph.D. in mathematics/education from the University of Connecticut. He has been at Westfield for twenty years teaching undergraduate courses in mathematics and computer science, conducting seminars for middle and secondary teachers, and supervising student teachers. Previous to his college teaching, he taught at the high school and junior high school levels. Dr. Edwards has conducted state and national workshops on mathematics and thinking skills and has authored numerous articles and books in mathematics/education and applications of mathematics.

ACKNOWLEDGEMENT

The authors and publisher are grateful to David Lance Goines and his publisher, David R. Godine, Incorporated, of Boston, for permission to use Mr. Goines' design on the cover of this book (from *A Constructed Roman Alphabet: A geometric analysis of the Greek and Roman capitals and of the Arabic numerals*, © 1982).

Table of Contents

MEASUREMENT

RELATIONS

TABLES AND GRAPHS

EXTENDING ACTIVITY MASTERS

Preface to Mathematical Reasoning

Objective

MATHEMATICAL REASONING, BOOK-1 introduces children in the lower elementary grades to the application of analytical and critical thinking skills within the study of mathematics. The primary goal of this book is not to teach students a set of arithmetic skills, but to encourage them to develop analysis and reasoning skills applicable to a wide range of mathematical concepts.

The activities presented in the book encourage students to develop investigative, analysis, and discussion abilities. The activities explore a variety of quantitative and spatial relationships that form the foundations of mathematics. The system of whole numbers and elementary geometry are used in the activities as vehicles to promote the development of these numerical and spatial concepts.

MATHEMATICAL REASONING, BOOK-1 consists of 1436 individual exercises on 282 reproducible student activity sheets arranged in six sections. These sections address six major strands in the elementary mathematics curriculum:

Number and Numeration
Geometry
Operations
Measurement
Relations
Tables and Graphs

The first two sections develop an understanding of basic number and geometric concepts. The remaining four sections build upon these number and spatial understandings and investigate their relationships and applications in problem solving. To be used most effectively, the materials should be followed sequentially. The presentation of the activities in each section assumes students have been exposed to the key concepts developed in earlier sections.

The MATHEMATICAL REASONING, BOOK-1 activities are compatible with the proposed standards for the school mathematics curriculum for grades K–4 as described in *Curriculum and Evaluation Standards for School Mathematics* (working draft), developed by the National Council of Teachers of Mathematics (NCTM), 1987.

The Role of the Teacher

For students to gain the maximum value from the MATHEMATICAL REASONING activities, it is important that the teacher understands and appreci-ates the role of investigation and verbal analysis when using these activities. To this end, this TEACHER'S MANUAL presents a series of suggestions and questions designed to focus and encourage student discussion through the use of mathematical ideas included in the exercises.

The activities in MATHEMATICAL REASONING, BOOK-1 and the suggestions in this TEACHER'S MANUAL provide teachers with an opportunity to teach students to *think mathematically*. The teacher's role is changed from reciting or explaining mathematical concepts to encouraging learners to explore and interact with these concepts. The teacher is encouraged to employ questioning techniques and discussion strategies which attempt to help learners move in a desired direction rather than providing a set of correct answers. The role of the teacher then becomes one of developing questioning techniques that allow students to "wrestle" with the task of explaining their reasoning—and providing ample opportunities for them to do so.

As a corollary to questioning techniques, the teacher must also develop acute listening skills. When an inappropriate response is given, it is often a delicate task to "hear" a student's reasoning, then rechannel it toward an appropriate response. The teacher must continually be aware that there may be more than one correct response in some situations. In fact, it may be more appropriate in many cases to think in terms of a "best" response rather than a correct or incorrect response. Unanimous agreement on the best answer is not crucial. It is crucial, however, that each person understands and appreciates the other's reasoning.

In the case of an unexpected response, the teacher should focus on the student's verbalized explanation or rationale for the answer before discussing its correctness. For example, a typical teacher reaction to an unexpected response might be, "Why did you choose that answer?"

In sum, the role of the teacher is not to put forth a body of information, but rather to serve as a catalyst between students' intuitive responses and their ability to offer a verbal rationale for their conclusions.

The Role of the Student

MATHEMATICAL REASONING, BOOK-1 uses mathematical concepts to foster logical reasoning development in students. A student's understanding of the role of logical relations in mathematics is dependent upon his or her ability to verbalize and explain an underlying mathematical process rather than providing a simple response to an exercise. To achieve the objective of thinking mathematically, students must become active participants in the learning process.

The objective of the material is to focus attention on this process rather than on attainment of an answer. In fact, in many cases it is assumed that students are able to obtain solutions to the exercises without difficulty, affording the teacher the opportunity to encourage discussion and explain the reasoning used to determine these solutions. Frequently, students are asked not only to analyze the mathematical concept underlying a given exercise, but to compare and analyze an entire set of exercises, to describe generalizations, and to make inferences concerning more general mathematical concepts and properties.

Each activity in MATHEMATICAL REASONING, BOOK-1 is designed to focus student attention on the tasks of examining, discussing, and describing numerical and geometric relationships in terms of logical relations. These logical relations include:

> analyzing similarities and differences

> recognizing sequences and patterns

> using numerical and spatial concepts for classification

> applying the concept of analogies to relations and functions

In addition, many activities stress using inductive reasoning to extend patterns, make predictions based upon available data, and formulate inferences. The role of deductive reasoning is introduced to students through the use of logical connectives, counterexamples, and the application of the process of elimination to derive solutions to numerical and geometric problems.

The presence of multiple solutions to certain exercises encourages students to realize that mathematics does not necessarily restrict itself to a single simple solution or a single strategy to arrive at a solution. The need to share ideas and compare solutions is of paramount importance. Such analysis and verbalizing results in students developing an appreciation that mathematics is indeed a logical discipline with recognizable patterns, order, and structure.

Mathematical Reasoning Program Elements

The MATHEMATICAL REASONING program consists of two elements designed to work together as one unit: 1) a teacher's manual and 2) a student activity book.

The Teacher's Manual

The TEACHER'S MANUAL provides introductory overviews for each of the six major sections of MATHEMATICAL REASONING, BOOK-1. The purpose of the overviews is to:

– stress the scope of the mathematical ideas presented in these sections

– provide suggestions to the teacher for presenting the material and becoming an active participant in the learning process

– present special notes on mathematical reasoning

– describe supplementary materials which may assist in exploring the ideas incorporated in the student activity sheets

In addition, each group of activities within a major section has a listing of the mathematical concepts addressed. These concepts can be related to topics in the scope and sequence of a standard mathematics textbook.

The TEACHER'S MANUAL also provides a commentary for each activity in the student book. This commentary includes a discussion of the mathematical concepts addressed and describes the interrelationships of the exercises on each activity page. The commentary also outlines the role of the teacher and suggests appropriate questioning techniques to lead and focus student investigations. Further, the commentary discusses strategies students may use in solving problems and makes reference to manipulative materials which may be used to facilitate or enhance the development of the mathematical concepts underlying the activity.

Solutions are given for each exercise, including reductions of completed student activity pages where they facilitate checking the student's work.

The Student Activity Book

The Table of Contents to MATHEMATICAL REASONING, BOOK-1 indicates that its six major sections are subdivided into groups of activities (with 2–10 activity sheets per group). These activities are organized around key mathematical ideas related to topics in a scope and sequence of standard mathematics textbooks used in the lower elementary grades.

The MATHEMATICAL REASONING program activities can also be used in conjunction with other materials in the Midwest Publications Analytic and Critical Thinking Program, or as a separate program to teach analytic and critical thinking in the elementary curriculum.

Although these topics can be related to a scope and sequence, it is important to note that the activity sheets should not be viewed as worksheet tasks for the learner to complete or as mere supplements to a standard mathematics textbook. The student activity sheets are intended to be used as a means of encouraging students to apply specific reasoning skills to mathematics and to verbalize the reasoning and strategies they might use in problem solving.

In addition, as previously stated, MATHEMATICAL REASONING, BOOK-1 encourages the use of other aspects of analytical and critical reasoning, including using inductive reasoning to make inferences and predictions based upon available data and employing deductive reasoning to derive logical solutions to mathematics problems.

The Role of Terminology

In most cases standard mathematical terminology appropriate to grade levels 2–4 is used throughout the student activity book and the TEACHER'S MANUAL. A few variations in terminology, however, should be noted.

In closed figures, right angles are referred to as square corners (page 79). The three geometric transformations—translations, rotations, and reflections—are identified as slides, turns, and flips (pages 89–91). The perimeter of a closed figure is referred to as the distance around a figure (page

189). Separating sets into nonoverlapping subsets is referred to as decomposition of sets (pages 117–122).

Supplementary Materials

Manipulatives

The TEACHER'S MANUAL to MATHEMATICAL REASONING, BOOK-1 includes several references to manipulative materials that might be used to encourage an understanding of the basic mathematical concepts in various activities.

Pattern blocks fit the diagrams on activity sheets 85, 106, 195, and 196. They are used to analyze and describe aspects of symmetry, the construction of figures by combining shapes, and in a discussion of perimeter.

Cuisenaire rods fit the diagrams on pages 63–68 which incorporate activities focusing on comparison of length.

Place value block reproductions are used on pages 47–62 to assist in developing an understanding of numeration.

Many other activities make reference to using *cubes*, *tiles*, *interlocking cubes*, *number-line models*, and *geoboards*. The commentary to specific activities in the TEACHER'S MANUAL contains suggestions for incorporating these materials into the MATHEMATICAL REASONING program.

Extending Activity Masters

Three useful reproducible forms appear at the end of this TEACHER'S MANUAL: **dot-paper designs** for geoboard exercises, **grid paper**, and **number-line models**.

These masters may be used for the trial and error experiments, guided practice, and extending activities suggested in this manual.

The Cognitive Model

Many activities in MATHEMATICAL REASONING, BOOK-1 have their origin in the cognitive development model delineated by Jean Piaget. A basic tenet of Piaget's cognitive model is that learning is an *interactive* process. Piaget maintained that the goal of education should be to provide the settings and opportunities for the learner to become actively involved in the learning process. He would have conjectured, in fact, that lectures or demonstrations are seldom useful with respect to a child's ability to understand a particular concept.

In a general sense Piaget would have maintained that learning and intellectual development are not passive, sporadic activities, but dynamic, ongoing processes. The ability to acquire knowledge is built upon the ability to organize and structure a concept's key components. Furthermore, this process is based upon the development of logical relationships. Thus, it is first necessary to identify those logical relationships that serve as the foundation of intellectual development, then to provide settings within an academic discipline that will enable a child to acquire proficiency with these relationships.

The application of logic and analysis skills to numerical and spatial concepts is introduced in MATHEMATICAL REASONING, BOOK-1. These basic reasoning skills include:

> examining similarities and differences between numerical quantities and geometric figures

> analyzing numerical sequences

> classifying numbers and geometric figures by properties

> applying the concept of analogies to mathematical relations and functions

A keystone of Piaget's cognitive development model is the concept of *operations*. An operation can be described as a tightly integrated system of thought processes that a child is able to apply to a concept or situation. These operations usually begin to emerge as a child reaches six to eight years of age, are cognitive in nature, internal, and not readily observable.

The task of riding a bicycle, which might be called a motor operation, can provide an appropriate analogy. If we can recall the complex motor skills and motor coordination involved in this activity, then we may begin to appreciate the complexity of a cognitive operation.

By carrying the comparison one step further and recalling Piaget's position on learning as an interactive process, we realize that the task of learning to ride a bicycle is not accomplished by reading a manual, listening to a lecture on the skill, and observing a demonstration of riding techniques. This task is truly a "learn-by-doing" activity.

In conjunction with the concept of an operation, Piaget defines four broad periods of intellectual development. The third period in the sequential development of cognition—*concrete operations*—is germane to the MATHEMATICAL REASONING activities.

Piaget characterizes the thinking processes associated with the concrete operations period as anchored to the real world. Children's thinking in this developmental period is generally restricted to a "before-the-eye" reality. Typically, the individual distrusts the hypothetical and is reluctant to become involved in situations that require generalizations and consideration of "what if..." questions.

Progress in intellectual development during this period is dependent upon providing a child with abundant opportunities to investigate, explore, analyze, and discuss situations that encourage development of the logical relationships discussed above. An understanding and appreciation of these relationships becomes the basis for development of abstract reasoning during the *formal operations* period.

The activities presented in MATHEMATICAL REASONING, BOOK-1 provide students with many opportunities to interact with these thinking skills within the context of numerical and spatial relations.

INTRODUCTION TO
NUMBER AND NUMERATION

The **Number and Numeration** section of **MATHEMATICAL REASONING** offers a wide variety of activities which are necessary for the development of a basic number sense in children. Much of the success of these activities is dependent upon the teacher becoming an active participant in the exploration and discussion of the mathematical concepts found in this section.

The teacher's role should be to encourage and assist students in developing and verbalizing strategies that can be used to analyze and understand the number concepts presented. The teacher should also assist students in devising strategies that can be used in solving the problems presented in the activities.

In addition, developing an understanding of the number concepts presented in the activities can often be facilitated by the use of manipulative materials. The teacher is encouraged to provide settings that incorporate the use of the appropriate manipulatives as students explore these mathematical ideas.

The activities in this section emphasize the discussion and analysis of three major mathematical ideas:

- counting
- comparison
- numeration

Counting activities are introduced in a variety of settings and are presented in conjunction with the number line, sets, and sequences. Students are encouraged to analyze and use several counting techniques, including consecutive counting (counting on and counting backward), skip counting

INTRODUCTION TO
NUMBER AND NUMERATION
(continued)

(multiples of 2, 3, and 5), and developing strategies for counting sets. In addition, several activities use counting to explore the concepts of ordering and comparing numbers.

Sets, lengths, and numbers are employed as vehicles to introduce the use of comparison as a mathematical tool. Comparing activities include using one-to-one correspondence (cardinality, equality, and inequality of sets) and counting strategies to compare lengths, regions, and number magnitude (equality and inequality). In addition, comparing densities is used as a method for estimating the relative size (cardinality) of sets.

The activities that explore the concept of numeration use a place-value model based upon cubes (units), rods (tens), and flats (hundreds). Activities that encourage students to discuss and analyze numeration and the properties of place value include grouping by tens, recording data, using expanded notation (composition and decomposition of sets), and using standard notation (face value and place value). As noted earlier, the teacher may find it beneficial to provide students with the appropriate manipulative materials and models to enhance the conceptual development of this important mathematical concept.

To further assist students, a page of reproducible number lines with different calibrations is included at the end of the manual. The number-line models can be used to provide additional insight into these concepts.

PAGES 1–6 COUNTING DOTS AND LETTERS

Mathematical Concepts
- Matching a set with a numeral (cardinality of sets)
- Consecutive counting
- Counting by multiples
- Sorting by a single attribute
- Developing problem-solving strategies

VERBAL ANALYSIS STRATEGIES AND ANSWERS

❑   PAGE 1: These exercises introduce the task of consecutive counting and the assigning of a number to a set of dots. Encourage the students to verbalize the differences between the various dot configurations. For example, A–1 and A–5 have the same number of dots on the diagonal, but A–1 has a dot in each of the four corners. A–2 and A–5 have dots in two of the four corners, but A–5 has an additional dot in the center of the square. Also compare A–3 and A–5, A–1 and A–3, the Example and A–1, etc., in terms of similarities and differences.

ANSWERS: **A–1** [5]   **A–2** [2]   **A–3** [1]   **A–4** [6]   **A–5** [3]

❑   PAGE 2: On this page the counting task is continued, and the idea of counting by multiples using vertical and/or horizontal patterns is introduced. Encourage the students to examine each exercise to determine whether a pattern for counting in multiples is present. A–7 can be viewed as four rows of six, or as six columns of four. A–8 contains a vertical pattern of two's, and A–10 has both vertical and horizontal patterns.

ANSWERS: **A–6** [15]   **A–8** [6]   **A–10** [12]
          A–7 [24]   **A–9** [12]

❑   PAGE 3: Dot patterns are used to further the concept of counting by multiples. Discuss the pattern in the Example (each square contains one more dot). In A–11 look for similarities (the sum of two squares in each row is 6) and differences (the two columns add up to 9 and 3). Students should verbalize the fact that the last four exercises on the page are similar. Each square within a particular exercise contains the same number of dots. Encourage the students to use counting by multiples to determine the total number of dots in A–13 (multiples of three), A–14 (multiples of five), and A–15 (multiples of two).

ANSWERS: **A–11** [12]   **A–13** [12]   **A–15** [8]
          A–12 [4]   **A–14** [20]

❑   PAGE 4: These exercises continue the use of multiples to count the number of elements in a set. Ask the students to circle the groupings of letters in the Example and in A–16 to A–20. Discuss with the students that A–19 and A–20 can be grouped by either columns or rows. Ask students to examine the similarities and differences among the patterns in the exercises. (Each grouping within an exercise has the same number of letters: A–16 has three in each group, A–17 has four in each group, etc.) Encourage the students to count in multiples to determine the total number of letters in each set. Ask them whether counting with horizontal patterns results in a different answer than counting with vertical patterns. Also compare A–18 and A–19 (same grouping of fives) and A–19 and A–20 (vertical groupings of threes have been increased).

ANSWERS: **A–16** [9]   **A–18** [15]   **A–20** [21]
          A–17 [16]   **A–19** [15]

❑   PAGE 5: The task of discriminating between letters and nonletters is introduced on this page. Discuss with the students what strategies might be used to simplify the task. For example, students might circle the letters prior to counting, or they might cross out the nonletters. Ask the students to determine whether any counting patterns exist within each set and whether horizontal or vertical counting procedures result in different answers.

ANSWERS: **A–21** [7]   **A–23** [9]   **A–25** [13]
          A–22 [8]   **A–24** [12]

❑   PAGE 6: This is a continuation of the discrimination activity introduced on page 5. Encourage the students to devise a strategy for eliminating the duplicate letters in each set. Discuss with the students the possibility of circling and crossing out letters to aid in the counting process. Also, ask the students to explain the patterns present in some exercises. In the Example all three rows have the same letters in different order (this is also true of A–27). In A–26 each letter is repeated with the group, while in A–28 there are two a's and one x in each column (also one less a and one more x in each row). Work with the students on A–30, which emphasizes the need for a counting strategy to determine the total number of different letters.

ANSWERS: **A–26** [9]   **A–28** [2]   **A–30** [10]
          A–27 [3]   **A–29** [6]

PAGES 7–10   COUNTING SEQUENCES OF LETTERS

Mathematical Concepts
- Matching a set with a numeral (cardinality)
- Consecutive counting
- Ordering letters of the alphabet
- Comparing sets: one-to-one correspondence
- Set, subset relationship

VERBAL ANALYSIS STRATEGIES AND ANSWERS

❑ PAGE 7: The activity of consecutive counting using sets of letters is continued. Compare A–31 with the Example. Some students may have to start with *a* to determine the missing letters in the sequences. Similarly compare A–33 with A–31. In A–34 and A–35 students may pair letters. Note that A–35 has two more letters than A–34, and A–34 has two more letters than A–33. Which sets of letters are equal?

ANSWERS: **A–31** [h, 9]   **A–34** [r, s, t, 7]   **A–37** [a, b, 5]
          A–32 [t, 4]   **A–35** [n, o, p, q, r, 9]
          A–33 [j, 5]   **A–36** [v, w, x, 7]

❑ PAGE 8: The task from page 7 is continued here with fewer cues. In A–41 students must list the letters in reverse order. Encourage students to compare exercises by pairing sets. A–43 and A–44 have the same number of letters, and A–45 has two more letters. Compare sets and, in particular, look at different lists that have the same number of letters.

ANSWERS: **A–38** [t, u, v, 5]   **A–42** [d, e, f, g, i, 6]
          A–39 [e, f, g, h, i, 8]   **A–43** [l, m, n, o, 5]
          A–40 [c, d, e, f, 6]   **A–44** [p, q, r, s, 5]
          A–41 [t, u, v, w, 7]   **A–45** [f, g, h, i, j, l, 7]

❑ PAGE 9: This page introduces the "three-dot" notation for continuing a pattern in a set. Emphasize that the three-dot notation does not always represent three missing letters. In A–46 some students may have to recite the alphabet starting with *a*. Encourage students to compare sets by matching elements to determine equal, smaller, and larger sets.

ANSWERS: **A–46** [f, g, h, i, 8]   **A–48** [o, p, q, r, s, 8]
          A–47 [s, t, u, 7]   **A–49** [m, n, o, p, q, r, 9]

❑ PAGE 10: More complex problems are added as the activity from page 9 is continued. Emphasize again to students that three dots does not mean three letters are missing. For example, compare A–50 and A–51. Also, in these exercises students are not asked to list the missing letters. However, some students may *need* to list the missing letters. Compare A–50 with the Example. Do they have letters in common? Compare A–53 through A–56. For example, A–54 has two fewer letters (*y, z*) than A–53. Note that A–54, A–55, and A–56 are subsets of A–53. Discuss why A–51 and A–52 are equal.

ANSWERS: **A–50** [5]   **A–53** [26]   **A–56** [22]
         A–51 [10]   **A–54** [24]
         A–52 [10]   **A–55** [24]

PAGES 11–14 COUNTING SEQUENCES OF NUMBERS

Mathematical Concepts
- Counting from a number different from one
- Consecutive counting
- Counting backward
- Comparing sets: one-to-one correspondence
- Set, subset relationships
- Finding a set to match a number

VERBAL ANALYSIS STRATEGIES AND ANSWERS

❑ PAGE 11: Number sequences are used in these exercises to carry forward the concepts from pages 7–10. Compare lists for subset relationships. For example, A–59 is a subset of A–58. Compare sets by matching elements. For example, A–61 and A–62 are different lists but have the same number of elements. Also, A–58 and A–60 have some elements in common and are the same size, which is also true for A–58 and the Example.

ANSWERS: **A–57** [3, 4 / 5]   **A–61** [25, 26 / 5]
         A–58 [9, 10, 11 / 6]   **A–62** [37, 38 / 5]
         A–59 [10, 11 / 4]   **A–63** [51, 52, 53, 54 / 6]
         A–60 [13, 14, 15 / 6]

❑ PAGE 12: This is a continuation of page 11, but with fewer cues. Counting backward is introduced, as for example in A–68, A–69, and A–70. Continue comparing sets with respect to similarities and differences. Note that A–65, A–66, A–68, A–69, and A–71 each have six elements. Which sets are disjoint (have no common elements)?

ANSWERS: **A–64** [7, 8 / 5]   **A–68** [14, 15, 16 / 6]
A–65 [12, 13, 14 / 6]   **A–69** [27, 28, 29 / 6]
A–66 [21, 22, 23, 24 / 6]   **A–70** [17, 18, 20, 21 / 5]
A–67 [32, 33, 35, 36, 37 / 7] **A–71** [10, 9 / 6]

❏ PAGE 13: The three-dot notation is reintroduced. Remind the students that three dots do not necessarily correspond to three numbers. Some students may need to start counting from 1. Again, encourage comparing lists. Compare A–72 and the Example by matching elements. A–72 has one more element. Continue this comparison for A–72, A–73, and A–74. Which sets are disjoint? Note that A–74 and A–75 are disjoint but have the same number of elements.

ANSWERS: **A–72** [6, 7, 8 / 7]   **A–74** [32, 33, 34, 35, 36, 37 / 9]
A–73 [14, 15, 16, 17 / 8] **A–75** [52, 53, 54, 55, 56, 57 / 9]

❏ PAGE 14: Here the tasks from pages 11–13 are reversed. Given the number of elements in a list and the beginning numbers in the list, students must identify the last number in the list. Most students will have to count consecutively from the beginning of the list. Assist students in developing a counting strategy (a number line may assist in this process). Extending the list and counting the elements may be necessary steps for some students. Compare the answers in A–76, A–80, and A–81.

ANSWERS: **A–76** [6]   **A–79** [15]
A–77 [17]   **A–80** [9]
A–78 [25]   **A–81** [20]

PAGES 15–20 COMPLETING NUMBER SEQUENCES

Mathematical Concepts
- Consecutive counting
- Counting backward
- Multiples of 2, 3, and 5
- Comparing sets: one-to-one correspondence
- Constructing sequences of numbers
- Identifying multiples of 2, 3, 5, and 10

VERBAL ANALYSIS STRATEGIES AND ANSWERS

❏ PAGE 15: This page introduces the task of continuing a sequence by consecutive counting from a number other than 1. Compare the Example with A–82. A–82 is a continuation of the sequence in the Example. Note that A–82 is a subset of A–83, and that A–83 has two more elements. Compare the unit digits in A–85 and A–88 (0, 1, 2,...). Note that A–85 has one more element than A–88. Do the same with A–84 and A–85. A–84 goes from 1 to 6 and A–85 from 0 to 6.

ANSWERS: **A–82** [20, 21, 22]   **A–86** [67, 68, 69]
                 A–83 [19, 20, 21, 22]   **A–87** [9, 10, 11, 12]
                 A–84 [54, 55, 56]   **A–88** [32, 33, 34, 35]
                 A–85 [93, 94, 95, 96]

❑ PAGE 16: These exercises extend the task from page 15 by having students count backward from a number. Compare A–93 and A–96 with respect to the unit digits. Why does A–93 have two more elements? Make a similar comparison between A–94 and A–95. Which has more elements? Note that A–89 is a continuation of the sequence in A–90.

ANSWERS: **A–89** [10, 9, 8]   **A–93** [39, 38, 37, 36]
                 A–90 [17, 16, 15]   **A–94** [7, 6, 5]
                 A–91 [90, 89, 88, 87] **A–95** [57, 56, 55, 54]
                 A–92 [35, 36, 37]   **A–96** [60, 59, 58]

❑ PAGE 17: The task of consecutive counting continues, but the missing numbers are not always in consecutive positions. Students must determine what comes before given numbers in a list. In some exercises (A–101 and A–103), students may have to count backward. Continue comparing unit digits in the sequences (A–100 and A–103). Also, compare the unit digits in the Example and A–101. Are the lists the same length? Note that A–101 is a continuation of A–97.

ANSWERS: **A–97** [5, 7, 9]   **A–101** [11, 12, 16]
                 A–98 [83, 86, 87] **A–102** [29, 31, 32, 34]
                 A–99 [18, 20, 21] **A–103** [15, 16, 18, 19]
                 A–100 [56, 57, 60, 61]

❑ PAGE 18: This page is similar to page 17 but focuses on counting backward. Continue comparing sequences. For example, compare the unit digits in A–108 and A–109. Also, note that A–109 is a continuation of the sequence in A–107. What number is needed to make A–108 a continuation of A–107? Similarly compare A–106 and A–107.

ANSWERS: **A–104** [95, 94, 90, 89] **A–108** [8, 7, 6, 3]
                 A–105 [83, 86, 87, 89] **A–109** [9, 7, 5, 4]
                 A–106 [21, 20]   **A–110** [45, 46, 49, 50, 51]
                 A–107 [16, 14, 12]   **A–111** [71, 70, 69, 67, 66]

❑   PAGE 19: Here sequences are introduced which are multiples of 2, 3, 5, or 10. Have students identify all the sequences that are multiples of 2 (then of 3, 5, and 10). Compare the multiples of 2 with respect to the unit digits (A–112 and the Example, and A–115). Also compare the unit digits in A–113 and A–118.

ANSWERS: **A–112** [8, 10, 12, 14]   **A–116** [70, 80, 90]
                  A–113 [15, 18, 21]   **A–117** [45, 50, 55, 60]
                  A–114 [20, 25, 30, 35]   **A–118** [39, 42, 45, 48]
                  A–115 [32, 34, 36]

❑   PAGE 20: This page has a mixture of sequences which involves consecutive counting, counting backward, and multiples of 2, 3, and 5. Missing numbers in the sequences are not always in consecutive positions. Again have students identify all the sequences which are multiples of 2 (the Example, A–122, and A–124). Do the same for multiples of 5 (A–120, A–121, and A–125). Continue to compare the unit digits in these sequences. How do A–119 and A–123 differ from the other sequences on page 20?

ANSWERS: **A–119** [6, 15]   **A–123** [17, 18, 20, 21]
                  A–120 [15, 20, 30, 35]   **A–124** [18, 12, 8]
                  A–121 [15, 20, 25, 35]   **A–125** [45, 40, 30, 25]
                  A–122 [4, 8, 12]

PAGES 21–22   PROPERTIES OF SETS OF NUMBERS

Mathematical Concepts
- Comparing sets: similarities and differences
- Defining a set by the properties of its elements
- Relationship between elements and sets
  (belong and not belong)

VERBAL ANALYSIS STRATEGIES AND ANSWERS

❑   PAGE 21: Given a set of numbers, students must identify the common properties of these numbers. Have students consider multiples (the Example is multiples of 10, A–126 is multiples of 5) or place value (A–128 represents even numbers in unit columns and A–127 has the number 6 in the tens place). Note that the elements in A–129 are all one-digit numbers. Encourage students to explain why the other three choices were not circled.

ANSWERS: **A–126** [b. 30]   **A–128** [b. 4]
            A–127 [c. 67]   **A–129** [b. 7]

❑ PAGE 22: The complementary task from page 21 is continued in this activity. Students must determine which element does not belong to each set; that is, what number does not share a common property with the other four numbers. The properties are similar to those on page 21. Encourage students to describe the sets by identifying the common properties, and discuss similarities and differences of the sets. (The Example has even numbers and A–135 has odd numbers.)

ANSWERS: **A–130** [46]   **A–133** [49]   **A–136** [64]
            A–131 [21]   **A–134** [21]
            A–132 [33]   **A–135** [6]

PAGES 23–24 COMPARING LENGTHS

Mathematical Concepts
- Counting squares
- Comparing numbers to ten
  (more than, less than, and equal to)
- Visually comparing lengths
- Comparing lengths by matching units

VERBAL ANALYSIS STRATEGIES AND ANSWERS

❑ PAGE 23: Students must find the lengths of rectangles by counting squares, then identify rectangles which have a length of more than ten. Students should note that the length in the Example is twelve. In A–137 students may count the squares or observe that this exercise has one less square than the Example. Since the left edges of the rectangles are in line, students may find lengths by comparing individual exercises. (Note that A–138 is three squares shorter than A–137.) Discuss the relationship between sizes. Which is longest? Which is shortest? If Cuisenaire rods are available, students may compare their answers to the orange rod, which is ten centimeters long.

ANSWERS: Shade the following rectangles: **A–137**   **A–139**   **A–142**

❑ PAGE 24: The edges of the rectangles on this page are not always lined up. Note that the Example has nine squares. Discuss with the students that only rectangles of the same length or shorter should be shaded. Students can still rely upon counting, but some rectangles are visually shorter than others (A–145 is obviously shorter than the Example). The edges of A–144, A–146, A–148, and A–150 are lined up, making comparison easier. Note that A–149 and A–150 are equal in length.

ANSWERS: Shade the following rectangles: **A–145   A–149**
                                                                    A–147   A–150

PAGES 25–28 COMPARING SETS

Mathematical Concepts
* Matching a set with a numeral (cardinality)
* Comparing sets by matching elements
* Visually comparing sets by comparing density
* Estimating the number in a set
* Counting techniques
* Problem-solving strategies

VERBAL ANALYSIS STRATEGIES AND ANSWERS

❑ PAGE 25: Students are asked to compare the cardinality of sets. Discuss three strategies: counting dots, matching dots in two sets by crossing out corresponding pairs (where a pair includes one dot from each set), or visual comparison by examining the density. In the Example, Set A has ten dots and Set B has six dots. In A–152, after seven pairs of dots are crossed out, Set B has four dots left. In A–151 and A–153, Set B appears to have many more dots. Have students try the above three strategies in the exercises. Also, have them examine the answers and determine which set on the page has the largest number of dots.

ANSWERS: **A–151** [Set B]   **A–152** [Set B]   **A–153** [Set B]

❑ PAGE 26: This page continues the activity from page 25. Encourage students to select their answers by visually comparing densities and to check their answers by counting or matching. Of the eight sets on the page, which has the least number of dots? (Set A in A–154 and Set B in A–155 are equal.) Which has the largest number of dots? (Set B in A–154 and Set B in A–156 are equal.)

ANSWERS: **A–154** [Set B]   **A–156** [Set B]
                   A–155 [Set A]   **A–157** [Set A]

❑ PAGE 27: Here students are asked to match a set to a set of equal size from four choices. Students may again use counting, matching elements, or estimation. Clearly, A–158 has three elements and the answer is obvious. In A–159 counting is necessary. Encourage students to use earlier counting techniques (for example, five rows of five dots each). After completing A–159, A–160 can be matched by estimation. If students do the exercises in order, A–161 can be matched by elimination. Students may then compare and discuss the densities of the ten sets on the page.

ANSWERS:

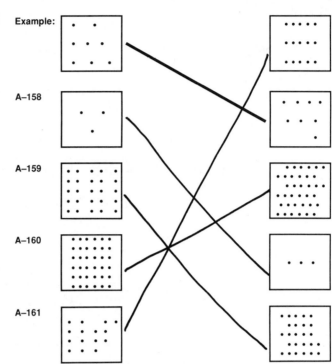

❑ PAGE 28: In these exercises the matching sets are not exactly the same size, but counting is still a possible strategy. Encourage students to estimate. For example, exercise A–163 may be done first. It is the most dense set in the exercises and matches the top set in the right column. Also, A–164 has five dots and should be matched with the set of four dots. Have students discuss and compare strategies in each exercise, then have them verify their answers by counting. Of the ten sets on the page, which is the most (or least) dense?

ANSWERS:

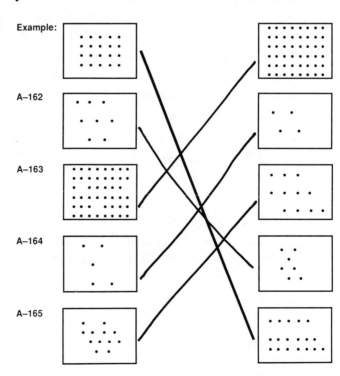

PAGES 29–32 COMPARING REGIONS

Mathematical Concepts
- Strategies for comparing regions
- Quantitative:
  counting parts of a region
  comparing fractional parts
  ordering fractional parts (more, less)
- Visual:
  comparing fractional parts

VERBAL ANALYSIS STRATEGIES AND ANSWERS

❑ PAGE 29: Using the strategy of counting equal parts of regions, these exercises introduce the part-whole relation (fractions). Stress the need to count both shaded and unshaded regions to determine the total. Compare A–166 and A–167 to the Example using one less and one more region shaded. Compare A–168 through A–170 in terms of one less region and an equal number of regions shaded. Also, note that A–170 and the Example have the same amount of shading (one half of the circle is shaded). The same is true for A–168. Which exercises have less than one half of the circle shaded?

ANSWERS: **A–166** [1, 4]   **A–168** [4, 8]   **A–170** [4, 8]
        A–167 [3, 4]   **A–169** [3, 8]

❑ PAGE 30: The activity from page 29 is continued using subdivisions of squares. Compare A–171 to A–172 in terms of which has more of the squares shaded. Note that both A–174 and A–175 have one-half of the squares shaded, while A–176 has less than one-half shaded. Note also that by rearranging the shaded squares in A–174, the same figure can be made as in A–175; or by re-arranging A–175, the same figure can be made as in A–174 . Also, A–173 could be subdivided into sixteen small squares and compared to A–174 and A–175.

ANSWERS: **A–171** [1, 4]   **A–173** [2, 4]   **A–175** [8, 16]
        A–172 [3, 4]   **A–174** [8, 16]   **A–176** [6, 16]

❑ PAGE 31: This page continues the comparison of the shaded parts of a region to a whole region. Students are asked to identify which shadings represent more than (or less than) one-half of the circle. Discuss with the students the strategy of drawing a model where one-half of the circle is shaded. Then have them visually compare the exercises to the model. Suggest that students compare, by counting regions, exercises A–178 and A–181 (the same number of regions are shaded) and the Example and A–179.

ANSWERS: **A–177** [Less]   **A–179** [More]   **A–181** [More]
           A–178 [More]   **A–180** [Less]

❑ PAGE 32: In these exercises the equal subdivision lines are missing. The students must make visual comparisons to a circle where one-half is shaded. Students may again draw a model for comparison. Another strategy would be to extend a radius to create a half circle, as in the Example, A–182, and A–183. Have students compare A–182, A–184, and A–186. Which has the largest part of the circle shaded? (A–182) Also, compare the Example and A–185. Do they appear to have the same amount of shading? (Yes.)

ANSWERS: **A–182** [More]   **A–184** [More]   **A–186** [More]
           A–183 [Less]   **A–185** [Less]

PAGES 33–40   USING THE NUMBER LINE

Mathematical Concepts
- Locating whole numbers on the number line
- Consecutive counting
- Counting backward
- Ordering numbers on the number line
- Overlapping sets
- Betweenness property on the number line

VERBAL ANALYSIS STRATEGIES AND ANSWERS

❑ PAGE 33: This page begins a series of activities using the number line. Not all of the number lines begin at zero; therefore, some students may need to refer to the Example, which does start at zero. Discuss with the students the overlap of the number lines in the Example, A–187, and A–188. What is the relationship between the number lines in A–188 and A–189? In A–190 students may have to count backward to complete the first two boxes. Discuss the sequence of numbers in the unit digits in exercise A–190.

ANSWERS: **A–187** [6, 7, 8, 9]   **A–189** [19, 20, 21, 24, 25]
           A–188 [11, 12, 13, 14, 15, 16] **A–190** [31, 32, 34, 35]

❑   PAGE 34: The activity from page 33 continues, but in all exercises except A–193 students will be required to count backward to begin each number line. Ask students to look for number lines which overlap.

ANSWERS: **A–191** [5, 6, 7, 11, 12]
                A–192 [18, 19, 20, 24, 25]
                A–193 [18, 19, 20, 21, 22]
                A–194 [33, 34, 35, 36, 37]
                A–195 [51, 52, 53, 54, 56, 57, 58]

❑   PAGE 35: Consecutive counting is used in these exercises to locate a particular number on the number line. Some students may have to write the complete sequence of whole numbers to the position of the missing number. Others may use counting backward as a strategy to locate the number (as in the Example, A–196, A–197, and A–198). Ask students to compare the number lines in A–197 and A–198. (They are the same.) Then have them compare the unit digits in number lines A–198 and A–199. Observe the different spacing used in the number lines in the Example and in A–196 compared with the rest of the exercises.

ANSWERS: **A–196** [29]   **A–197** [11]   **A–198** [7]   **A–199** [36]

❑   PAGE 36: In these exercises students are asked to determine the number value of a particular location when they are given only one value on the number line. Students must use consecutive counting or counting backward in A–202 and A–203. Some students may have to write the complete sequence of numbers on the number line between boxes. Discuss with students how far the answer is from the given number. Note that in the Example, A–201, and A–202 the answer is five away from the given value. How does this compare with A–200 and A–203?

ANSWERS: **A–200** [37]   **A–201** [65]   **A–202** [5]   **A–203** [22]

❑   PAGE 37: Students are asked to position four given numbers on a number line where one or more numbers are given as cues. Some students may use consecutive counting, while others may order the four given values to locate the missing numbers on the number line. Discuss this latter strategy with students; that is, the smallest number in the set goes in the first box, the next largest in the second box, etc. Have students consider overlap of the sets. Note that A–206 is a continuation of A–204, and that the Example and A–205 overlap in a single point (8).

ANSWERS: **A–204** [3, 5, 6, 10]   **A–206** [11, 12, 15, 16]
                A–205 [9, 12, 13, 15]

❑   PAGE 38: This page extends the previous set of exercises, with no reference numbers given on the number lines. Here students must use the strategy discussed on page 37. Discuss the relationship (overlapping) of the first three exercises. Note that no two number lines begin at the same value (A–209 begins at 10). At what value does each of the other number lines begin?

ANSWERS: **A–207** [3, 7, 9, 12]   **A–209** [10, 12, 17, 24]
                   A–208 [5, 10, 12, 15]   **A–210** [32, 34, 36, 40]

❑   PAGE 39: Each number line has at least two reference points. Note that the values of the left and right endpoints are not always given. In each exercise ask students to determine the values of the endpoints. Then have them determine which of the four given numbers cannot be located on that line. Ask students if their selection is too large or too small to fit on the line. Students should then verify that the other numbers do fit on the line by locating their positions.

ANSWERS: **A–211** [c. 7]   **A–213** [a. 21]   **A–215** [d. 60]
                   A–212 [b. 21]   **A–214** [c. 58]

❑   PAGE 40: This page is a continuation of page 39. Each number line is identical (beginning at 10 and ending at 30). Note that there may be more than one of the four given values that does not fit on the number line. Have students tell why their choices don't fit (they are less than 10 or more than 30). Also, have them verify that the other numbers do fit on the number line. Discuss the properties of the numbers that fit on the number line from 10 to 30—e.g., all the numbers in the 20's.

ANSWERS: **A–216** [c. 33, d. 40] **A–218** [a. 50] **A–220** [c. 34]
                   A–217 [b. 43, d. 6]   **A–219** [a. 34]

PAGES 41–46   COMPARING NUMBERS

Mathematical Concepts
- Differences between numbers
- Closeness on the number line
- Comparing numbers (greater than, less than)
- Betweenness
- Set/subset relationship
- Describing a set by the properties of its elements

VERBAL ANALYSIS STRATEGIES AND ANSWERS

❑   PAGE 41: These exercises introduce the concept of the relative position of numbers on the number line. Discuss two possible strategies to answer the exercises. First, locate the given number on a number line and determine which of the five numbers is closest to that number. Second, compare the differences between the given value and the five choices. In the Example, the difference between the given value (7) and the answer (8) is one. Ask students to compare the differences in each exercise. There is a difference of one in A–221 and A–222. There is a difference of two in the remaining exercises.

ANSWERS: **A–221** [5]   **A–223** [8]   **A–225** [27]
          A–222 [11]   **A–224** [14]

❑   PAGE 42: This activity extends the exercises on page 41. The nearest number is sometimes greater than the given number and sometimes less than the given number. Discuss the two strategies used on page 41. The answer in A–226 is one less than 5. Ask the students what number would be that close to, but more than, 5. Ask similar questions about the remaining exercises. Note that in A–227 through A–231 the answer is always two more or less than the given number.

ANSWERS: **A–226** [4]   **A–228** [16]   **A–230** [25]
          A–227 [12]   **A–229** [7]   **A–231** [61]

❑   PAGE 43: The task of comparing the numbers in a set to a given number is introduced here. (Which numbers are greater than the given number?) Discuss that some sets (A–233, A–235, and A–236) contain values equal to the given number. Note that these numbers should not be circled. Discuss that the circled numbers form a subset of the number in the square. Ask students to verbalize the property of this subset. Also, have them describe the properties of the uncircled numbers in the box. (The numbers are less than or equal to the given number.) Note that in each subset, the largest value is marked with an X.

ANSWERS: **A–232** [10, 20, 12, 16, 13,   X on 20]
          A–233 [11, 20, 4, 9, 6,   X on 20]
          A–234 [15, 12, 32, 20, 41,   X on 41]
          A–235 [90, 70, 80, 60,   X on 90]
          A–236 [28, 36, 42, 25,   X on 42]

❑   PAGE 44: This activity is similar to that on page 43, but uses the property *less than*. Again, note that the given value appears in some sets (A–237, A–240, and

A–241); discuss the properties of the subsets (circled numbers) and the properties of the uncircled numbers. Ask students to order the circled numbers from smallest to largest in each exercise.

ANSWERS: **A–237** [4, 5, 0, 7,   X on 0]
                A–238 [9, 12, 14, 10, 8, 0,   X on 0]
                A–239 [29, 32, 20, 19,   X on 19]
                A–240 [35, 60, 75, 55, 70, 65,   X on 35]
                A–241 [44, 39, 27, 40,   X on 27]

❏   PAGE 45: Comparing numbers using the betweenness property is introduced in this activity. Only numbers strictly greater than the first given number and less than the second number should be circled. Note that the given number(s) appears in some sets. For example, both 4 and 8 appear in A–243 and should not be circled. Discuss the properties of the circled and the uncircled numbers in each set. Compare A–242 and A–244. Ask students if all the numbers between the given values are listed in the set.

ANSWERS: **A–242** [6, 5, 4]   **A–245** [12, 14, 13]
                A–243 [7, 6, 6, 7]   **A–246** [28, 30, 27, 31]
                A–244 [9, 7, 6, 10]

❏   PAGE 46: This is a continuation of page 45 using the betweenness property. DIscuss again the properties of the subsets and whether all of the *between* values are in the set. Ask the students to describe other properties of the circled numbers in A–249 and A–250 in terms of multiples.

ANSWERS: **A–247** [14, 15]   **A–250** [25, 30, 20]
                A–248 [16, 14, 17]   **A–251** [68, 59]
                A–249 [25]   **A–252** [39, 43, 41, 35]

PAGES 47–62   PLACE VALUE

Mathematical Concepts
- Grouping by tens
- Matching sets of ten with lengths of ten
- Collecting and organizing data
- Place value (standard notation)
- Face value and place value of digits

VERBAL ANALYSIS STRATEGIES AND ANSWERS

❑ PAGE 47: Here begins a series of activities dealing with place value and grouping by ten. Place-value blocks serve as a model to develop these concepts. Discuss with students that each rod pictured consists of ten cubes. If available, the manipulatives (place value blocks) may be used in conjunction with this series of activities. When discussing students' solutions, note that there are many different ways groups of ten may be arranged. Discuss the strategy of putting X's on blocks until ten are counted. Then circle that group of ten. Ask students comparison questions about the sets in the left column, such as which has the largest number of cubes, etc.? The same may be done for the sets in the right column. Discuss the difference between the top and bottom sets (32 cubes and 23 cubes).

❑ PAGE 48:   ANSWERS: This page extends the activity of page 47, with flats consisting of one hundred cubes or ten rods introduced. Grouping still involves the grouping of ten cubes to make a rod. Again, have students compare the relative sizes of the sets pictured in the exercises and their matching sets. Which sets have the largest or smallest number of cubes? Note, as mentioned above, that each rod consists of ten cubes.

ANSWERS:

Example:

A–253

A–254

A–255

A–256

A–257

A–258

A–259

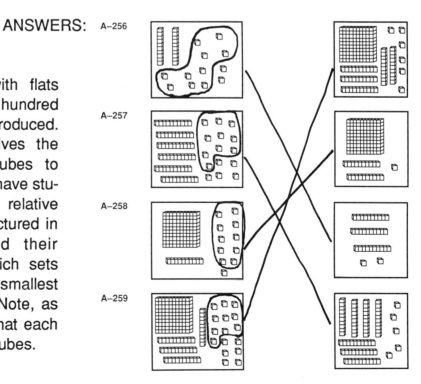

❑ PAGE 49: No grouping is required in these exercises. Students are asked to count the number of rods and the number of ungrouped cubes in a set, and to match their results to data in a table. Discuss the difference between the tables for A–261 and A–262. (One is 56 and the other is 65.) Have students compare the relative sizes of sets. For example, A–260 is larger than A–261. Stress that each rod contains ten cubes.

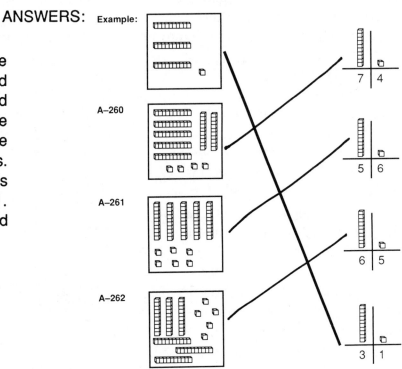

❑ PAGE 50: This is an extension of the activity on page 49. Here cubes, rods, and flats (of one hundred cubes) are used in a similar activity. Note that only the numbers 1, 2, and 3 are used in the matching tables. This differentiates between place value and face value. Discuss the strategy of first counting flats, then rods, and finally separate cubes. Note the variation in the placement of the flats, rods, and cubes within the sets.

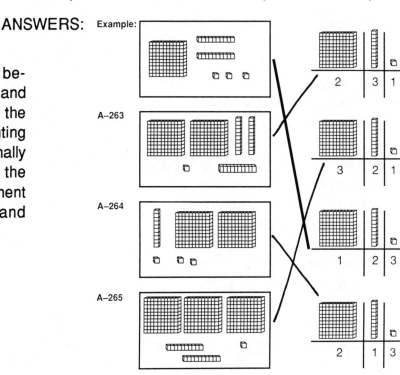

❑   PAGE 51: The transition from recording numbers in a table to writing numbers in standard notation is completed in these exercises. Here students must first fill in the data table, then use the table to write numbers in standard notation. Discuss the strategy of counting rods first, then cubes. Again, have students compare sizes of sets using the given sets, the data tables, and the circled numbers. For example, which set has the larger number of cubes, A–266 or A–267? What is meant by more cubes?

ANSWERS: **A–266** [38]   **A–267** [53]   **A–268** [41]

❑   PAGE 52: This page continues the previous activity and incorporates flats into the given sets. Discuss strategies of counting and recording data in the table. Each set contains one flat. Also, sets A–269 through A–271 contain five rods. Discuss the arrangements of flats, rods, and cubes in the exercises. Note that the value *zero* is introduced in A–271 (there are no separate cubes). Have students compare the sizes of the sets pictured in A–269 to A–271.

ANSWERS: **A–269** [153]   **A–270** [156]   **A–271** [150]

❑   PAGE 53: These exercises bypass the step of using a data table. Students match sets of cubes with the number of cubes written in standard notation. Some students may find it necessary to construct a data table before matching. Have students compare A–273 and A–274 (the difference between 62 and 26) with respect to place value. Continue to compare the sizes of sets.

ANSWERS: **A–272** [78]   **A–273** [62]   **A–274** [26]

❑   PAGE 54: The exercises on this page are similar to those on page 53, but use flats in the sets. Discuss counting strategies and the comparison of sets. Zero appears in both the units (A–278) and tens (A–277) place. Some students may need to make a data table as a transition to standard notation.

ANSWERS: **A–275** [235]   **A–277** [207]
                  A–276 [143]   **A–278** [130]

❑   PAGE 55: These exercises reverse the activity from page 54. Given a number in standard form, students must construct a set with that number of cubes. Discuss with students which digit in the Example (43) represents rods and which cubes. Again, some students may need to refer to a data table. Discuss a strategy for selecting rods and cubes. For example, select rods first, cubes last. Note that when discussing solutions, the number of X's should match, but they may appear on different rods or cubes. (The Example requires seven X's: four on rods and three on cubes.)

ANSWERS:

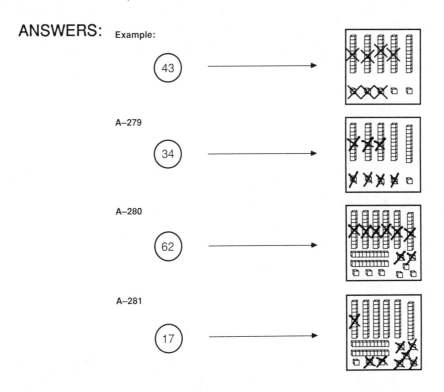

Example:

43

A–279

34

A–280

62

A–281

17

❑ PAGE 56: The activity from page 55 is continued, using three-digit numbers and selecting flats, rods, and cubes. The first three exercises focus on the concept of face value and place value of the digits 1, 2, and 3. Discuss which digits represent flats, rods, and cubes. Continue discussing strategies for constructing sets. Solutions may appear different, but the number of X's on flats, rods, and cubes must be the same in each student's answer. Discuss the presence of zero in A–285.

ANSWERS:

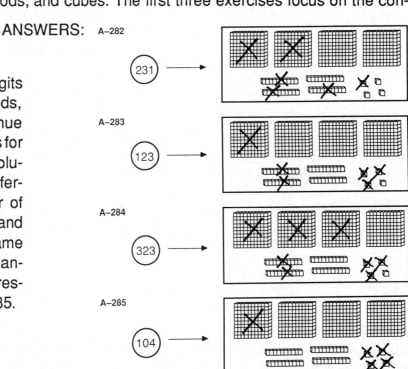

A–282

231

A–283

123

A–284

323

A–285

104

❑   PAGE 57: Sets are not pictured on this page, but students are told how many rods and how many separate cubes appear in each set. (Remind students that there are ten cubes in each rod.) Students again use this information to fill in a data table and write the results in standard notation. If manipulatives are available, actual sets may be constructed for each exercise. Have students compare the sizes of the sets represented. Does A–287 or A–288 have more cubes?

ANSWERS: **A–286** [62]   **A–287** [94]   **A–288** [39]

❑   PAGE 58: Flats, rods, and cubes are used to continue the activity from page 57. However, in exercises A–290 and A–291 the placement of flats, rods, and cubes differs from the Example and A–289. Discuss with students how this affects the entry of data in the data table. If manipulatives are available, they may be useful in these latter exercises. Continue comparing sets.

ANSWERS: **A–289** [359]   **A–290** [489]   **A–291** [637]

❑   PAGE 59: This continues the previous set of exercises, with the data table eliminated. However, to assist in these exercises, adding the data table or using manipulatives may be helpful. Continue to reinforce that each rod contains ten cubes. Also, stress that the answer to the Example (35) can be viewed as three rods and five cubes, or as thirty-five individual cubes. Compare the use of the digits 3 and 5 in the Example and A–293 (also, 5 and 7 in A–292 and A–294).

ANSWERS: **A–292** [a. 57]   **A–293** [a. 53]   **A–294** [a. 75]

❑   PAGE 60: Flats are included as the activity from page 59 is continued. Discuss the relationships among cubes, rods, and flats. Also, discuss the rearrangement of the sequence of flats, rods, and cubes in A–296 and A–297. Continue to discuss the relationships of face value and place value of the various digits. For example, if students circle b. 349 in exercise A–296, they are confusing place value and face value. The same is true in A–297.

ANSWERS: **A–295** [c. 123]   **A–296** [a. 439]   **A–297** [c. 762]

❑   PAGE 61: The tasks which appear on pages 59 and 60 are reversed here. Consider using manipulatives if they are available. Encourage students to verbalize the digits in terms of rods and cubes before recording the answers. This is especially important in A–299 and A–300 where the placement of rods and cubes has been reversed. Note that the digit 4 in A–299 represents cubes, whereas the 4 in A–300 represents rods.

ANSWERS: Example:

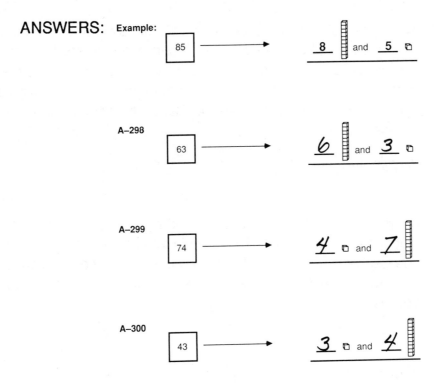

☐ PAGE 62: This page extends the activity on page 61 by including flats and three-digit numbers. Again, students should verbalize digits in terms of flats, rods, and cubes. Note the rearrangements in the figures for exercises A–303 and A–304.

ANSWERS: A–301

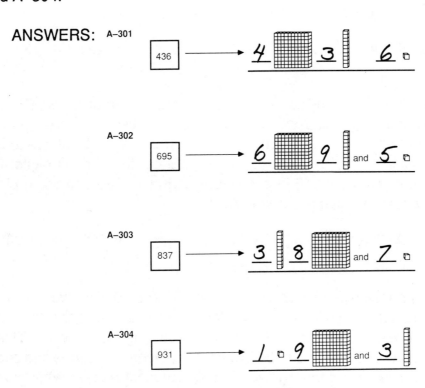

INTRODUCTION TO GEOMETRY

The **Geometry** section of **MATHEMATICAL REASONING** provides students with a variety of opportunities to explore the elementary properties of nonmetric geometry. These activities, combined with those from the **Number and Numeration** section, form the basis for analyzing the relationships between number and measurement that are considered in a later section.

This section explores three important geometric ideas:

- description and classification of shapes
- composition and decomposition of figures
- development of an elementary spatial sense

Several activities introduce students to the task of describing and classifying shapes. These activities are designed to emphasize the development of strategies that students may use as they compare lengths, determine congruence or similarity of figures, and investigate symmetric figures.

A geoboard model is used to introduce composition and decomposition activities. The model assists students in combining shapes to form new figures and in subdividing figures into nonoverlapping regions. As students discuss and verbalize the relationships between the results obtained in these exercises, the teacher should stress the existence of multiple solutions in many of the exercises, and stress the importance of these solutions as a mathematical construct.

The development of a spatial sense is dependent upon the ability of students to visualize and describe relationships between figures as they are moved and changed. Students begin to develop an understanding of these spatial concepts

P.O. BOX 448, PACIFIC GROVE, CA 93950

INTRODUCTION TO
GEOMETRY
(continued)

by analyzing and discussing activities involving the composition and decomposition of figures, by exploring the geometric properties of symmetry, and by visualizing and describing the attributes of the geometric motions (slides, turns, and flips).

The use of manipulative materials is important in developing an understanding of many elementary concepts in nonmetric geometry. Reference is made throughout the manual to specific materials that may be used to assist in the development of the underlying mathematical ideas within the individual activities. In addition, a reproducible page of geoboard designs appears at the end of this manual to aid in working the exercises.

PAGES 63–68 ESTIMATING LENGTHS

Mathematical Concepts
• Estimation
• Visual comparison of lengths
• Transitivity
• Strategies for comparing lengths

VERBAL ANALYSIS STRATEGIES AND ANSWERS

❑ PAGE 63: The task of visual comparison to a given length is introduced here. The rectangles in these activities allow Cuisenaire rods to be used, if they are available. (The given figure matches the ten-centimeter orange Cuisenaire rod.) Discuss with the students that the left edges of the figures are in line, making visual comparisons easier. Note that B–3 is the same length as the shaded figure and that this is not *less than*. Suggest that students verify their answers by either comparing the figures with an orange rod or lining a straight edge along the right edges of the given length and the figure in exercise B–3. Ask students which of the rectangles on the page is shortest and which is longest.

ANSWERS: Shade the following rectangles: **B–2   B–4   B–6   B–7**

❑ PAGE 64: This activity is similar to that on page 63, but the edges of the figures are no longer in line, making visual comparison and verification of answers more difficult. Visually, it should be clear to students that B–8, B–10, and B–12 are less than the given length. Also, B–9 and B–13 should be clearly greater than the given length. The relationship of B–11 and B–14 to the given length may not be clear. Discuss strategies for comparison. These may include using parallelism (connecting the edges with straight lines) or comparison to an orange rod. Measurement (with a centimeter ruler) should only be used to verify answers. The object of the exercise is to compare lengths visually and develop strategies for comparison, not to measure.

ANSWERS: Shade the following rectangles: **B–8   B–10   B–12   B–14**

❑ PAGE 65: Comparison continues, but using *greater than* a given length. On this page, the right edges of all the figures are aligned, and the given figure is five centimeters long (which corresponds to a yellow Cuisenaire rod). The rectangle in exercise B–19 is equal in length to the given figure and should not be shaded. After they complete the exercises, ask students to identify the shortest figure and the longest figure on the page. If Cuisenaire rods are available, they can be matched to the exercises and the Example, and placed in order of length. Are any rods not represented in the exercises, or do any appear more than once?

ANSWERS: Shade the following rectangles: **B–16   B–17   B–20**

❑ PAGE 66: This activity is similar to that on page 65, except that the edges are not aligned. Certain comparisons may be visually obvious to students (B–23 and B–28 are *greater than*, and B–22 and B–26 are *less than*). Discuss the strategies for comparing the given length with B–24, B–25, and B–27. Note that B–27 equals the given figure in length. Measurement in metric units should be used only to verify answers, not as a strategy to solve the exercises.

ANSWERS: Shade the following rectangles: **B–23   B–25   B–28**

❑ PAGE 67: This page introduces the relation *betweenness*. Each exercise must be compared to the two given lengths (greater than one and less than the other). Have students observe that the left edges of the figures are aligned. Discuss two complementary strategies: 1) eliminating lengths less than the five-centimeter figure (B–29 and B–31), and 2) eliminating lengths greater than the ten-centimeter figure (B–30 and B–33). Discuss with the students the properties of the remaining figures (the Example, B–32, and B–34). These are the answers. Why?

ANSWERS: Shade the following rectangles: **B–32   B–34**

❑ PAGE 68: In this extension of page 67, the edges of the figures are unaligned. The strategies from pages 64 and 66 may be used in conjunction with the strategy of elimination from page 67. Note that B–35, B–36, and B–38 would be eliminated. Ask students, "What are the properties of the remaining figures?"

ANSWERS: Shade the following rectangles: **B–37   B–39   B–40**

PAGES 69–76 COMPARING LENGTHS

Mathematical Concepts
- Estimation
- Comparing two or more lengths
- Transitivity
- Strategies for comparing lengths

VERBAL ANALYSIS STRATEGIES AND ANSWERS

❑ PAGE 69: This page continues the tasks from pages 63–68, with rectangles replaced by line segments. In the Example, B–41, and B–47, encourage the students to verbalize that two endpoints are aligned. Comparison then focuses on the other endpoints, as in the activities on pages 63 and 65. Discuss with students the relationship of endpoints in B–44, B–46, and B–48 (one set falls within the other). Discuss the relationship of endpoints in B–42, B–43, B–45, and B–49 (each pair of lines overlaps). Discuss two strategies for solving these exercises: 1) connect left endpoints and right endpoints and use parallelism, and 2) draw perpendiculars between segments from the two overlapping endpoints and compare the nonoverlapping parts of the segments.

ANSWERS:

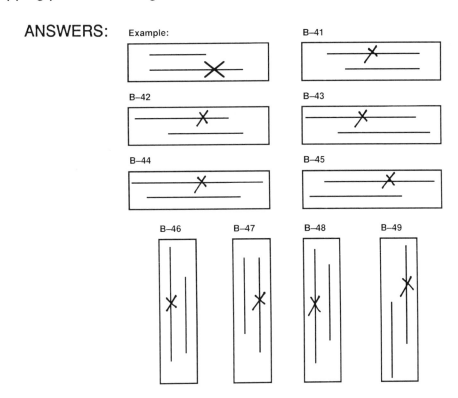

❑ PAGE 70: The activity from page 69 is extended to comparing three line segments. Discuss with students the relationship of endpoints. (Some exercises have three of their endpoints aligned, others two aligned, and others have their endpoints contained within other segments). Discuss alternative strategies for comparing three segments. For example, in B–56 one strategy may be: The left is longer than the middle when considering the aligned endpoints, and the left is also longer than the right segment since its endpoints are within those of the left segment. Another strategy is to use transitivity: The left is longer than the middle, and the middle longer than the right; therefore, the left is longer than the right.

ANSWERS:

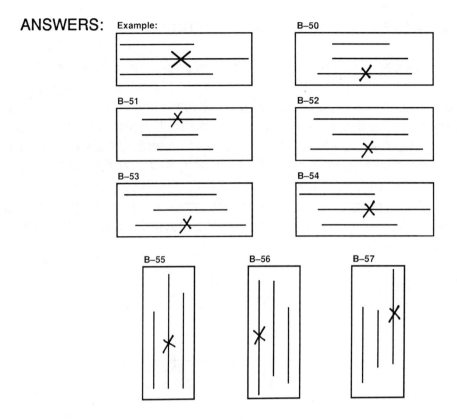

☐ PAGE 71: The development of the reasoning skills needed for comparison continues, with the comparison *longer* replaced by *shorter*. Further discuss with students the solution strategies that were used on pages 69–70.

ANSWERS:

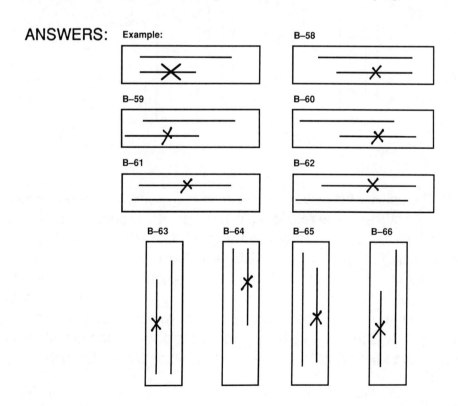

❑ PAGE 72: These exercises continue the reasoning concepts introduced on page 70, using *shortest* rather than *longest*. Continue to discuss the strategies used in the previous activities. For example, in B–67 reasoning by transitivity may be as follows: The top segment is shorter than the middle segment (aligned endpoints), and the middle segment is shorter than the bottom segment (aligned endpoints). Therefore, the top is shorter than the bottom, and thus is shortest. Also, the top segment could be compared to the bottom segment (the endpoints of the top are within the endpoints of the bottom).

ANSWERS:

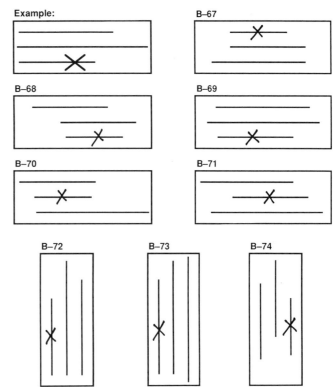

❑ PAGE 73: This continues the activity of comparing lengths using triangles (for three segments) and quadrilaterals (for four segments). Discuss strategies for determining the shortest side of a triangle, such as comparing pairs of sides. Strategies used in quadrilaterals may include comparing the parallel sides (endpoints aligned [B–76] or endpoints within [B–75 and B–80]). When comparing the shorter parallel side to an adjacent side, students may draw a diagonal to form a triangle. This allows them to use their previous experience of comparing sides within a triangle.

ANSWERS:

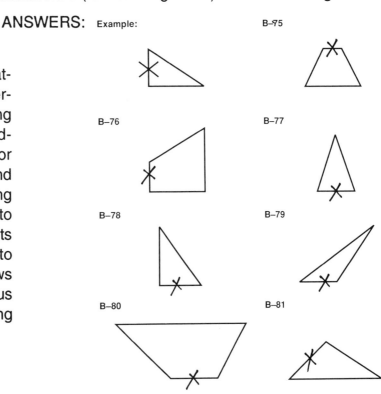

❏   PAGE 74: These exercises involve the comparison of a pair of segments. A comparing strategy that can be used in the exercises where there are angles involved is completing the triangle.

Then strategies from page 73 may be used, or some students may realize that the longest side of a triangle is always opposite the largest angle (and the shortest side is opposite the smallest angle). In B–84 and B–85, parallel lines can be drawn to make quadrilaterals.

ANSWERS:

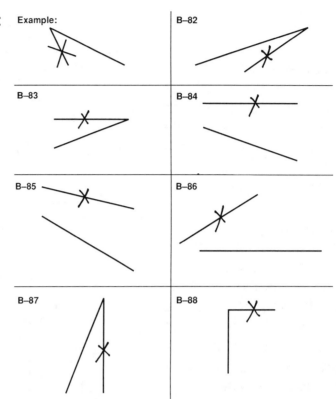

❏   PAGE 75: The activity from page 74 continues on this page, with *shortest* replaced by *longest*. Discuss first the strategy of comparison using the triangles.

Students should also be aware from the previous page that the longest side is opposite the largest angle. If not, you may want to lead them to this discovery. Compare the Example and B–92. The largest side is opposite the right angle. Note that the remaining triangles contain an obtuse angle. In the case of the quadrilaterals, review the strategies introduced on page 73.

ANSWERS:

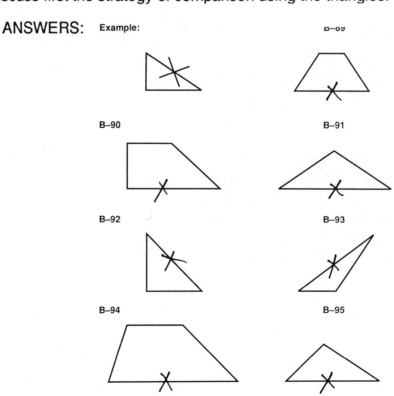

❑ PAGE 76: *Shorter* is replaced by *longer* in these exercises which follow the structure on page 74. Review the strategies discussed on page 74. Note that if a triangle is formed in B–98, the longest side would be the hypoteneuse. However, the comparison is between the two legs of the triangle.

ANSWERS:

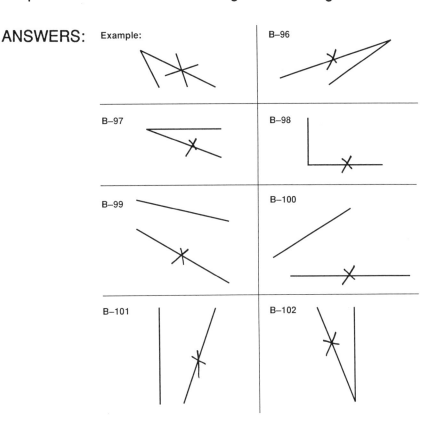

PAGES 77–82 CLASSIFYING BY SHAPE

Mathematical Concepts
- Classification of polygons using one or more attributes
- Logical connectives (and, or)
- Defining a set by the properties of its elements
- Union and intersection of sets
- Set/subset relationship
- Problem-solving strategies

VERBAL ANALYSIS STRATEGIES AND ANSWERS

❑ PAGE 77: After students classify the polygons (many-sided figures) by the number of sides, discuss the similarities and differences between triangles. For example, all have three sides, three vertices (points where two sides intersect), and three angles. Also, B–107 and B–109 are isosceles (each has a pair of equal sides), and B–108 is the only right triangle. Compare the remaining figures and discuss similarities and differences with regard to number of sides, types of angles, equality of sides, and parallel sides.

ANSWERS: Put an X on the following shapes: **B–107**   **B–108**   **B–109**

❑ PAGE 78: This activity continues the task from page 77. After students identify the quadrilaterals, have them discuss similarities and differences as suggested on page 77. For example, note that all figures on the page (with the exception of B–111) have at least one pair of parallel sides. Also, discuss similarities and differences between quadrilaterals with regard to the relationships of angles. For example, each has at least two equal angles. Note that B–113 has four equal angles, while B–116 has two pairs of equal angles. In addition, have students identify figures with one or more right angles.

ANSWERS: Put an X on the following shapes: **B–112**   **B–114**
                                           B–113   **B–116**

❑ PAGE 79: These exercises use two attributes for classification and stress the connective *and*. Discuss three possible strategies that could be used: 1) consider each shape individually—does it have three sides? Does it have a square corner? 2) identify all of the triangles first, then identify the subset with square corners; 3) identify the set of triangles first, then identify the set of figures with square corners and select the figures in the intersection of these two sets. Note in strategy 2 that figures with square corners could be identified first. Encourage students to verbalize why B–118, B–119, B–122, and B–123 were not selected.

ANSWERS: Put an X on the following shapes: **B–117**   **B–120**   **B–121**

❑ PAGE 80: The logical connective *or* in classification is stressed in this activity. After completing the exercises, have students verbalize the relationships between the selected figures with regard to the number of square corners. Does "one or more" square corners have the same meaning as "at least one" square corner? Explain why the other figures were not selected. Do the figures not selected have the same number of square corners?

ANSWERS: Put an X on the following shapes: **B–125**   **B–128**   **B–129**

❑ PAGE 81: Students must define a set using one or more attributes. Encourage students to consider common properties of the figures in the boxes, such as number of sides, types of angles, lengths of sides, and parallelism. The Example and B–131 may be solved using the single attribute, number of sides. More than one attribute must be used to solve B–132 and B–133. For example, in B–132 the exercise cannot be solved using simple number of sides, or equal angles, or parallel sides. The same is true for B–133. Have students verbalize similarities and differences between B–132 and B–133.

ANSWERS: Put an X on the following shapes: **B–131** [c]   **B–133** [c]
B–132 [b]

❑ PAGE 82: This page introduces the complementary activity to page 81. Encourage students to verbalize the common properties of the figures in the sets by classifying each figure according to number of sides, types of angles, lengths of sides, and parallelism. The discussion on page 81 that identified differences between rectangles and squares is necessary to solve the Example on this page. B–134 and B–135 are based on the single property, number of sides. However, a possible solution to B–135 would be to put an X on the third figure, if "one or more right angles" was used as the common property. The property of "one or more right angles" must be used to solve B–136.

ANSWERS:

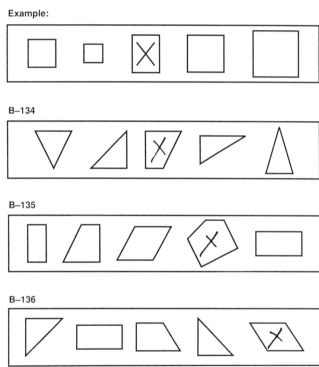

PAGES 83–88 SYMMETRY

Mathematical Concepts
- Symmetry
- Lines of symmetry
- Classifying figures using the attribute of symmetry

VERBAL ANALYSIS STRATEGIES AND ANSWERS

❏   PAGE 83: Here the task of finding lines of symmetry is introduced. Discuss with students the possibilities of both horizontal and vertical lines of symmetry.

Which figures have horizontal? Which vertical? Which have both? Note that B–140 and B–141 have both horizontal and vertical lines of symmetry. In addition, B–141 has two diagonal lines of symmetry. Students may discover or verify the lines of symmetry by folding the paper, tracing, and cutting. Manipulatives, such as pattern blocks, may also be used to illustrate symmetry.

ANSWERS:

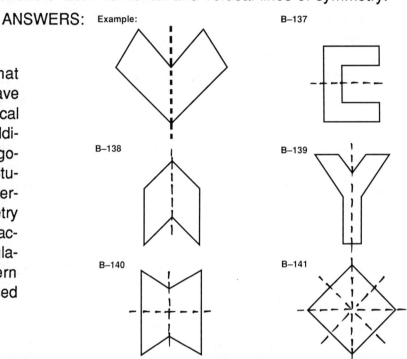

❏   PAGE 84: On this page students must distinguish symmetric and nonsymmetric figures. If students encounter difficulty in identifying symmetric figures, suggest they apply the strategies used on page 83.
Ask students to compare exercises B–142, B–146, and B–147. How are they similar? How are they different? Also, compare B–144 and B–151 and B–145 and B–152. Note that B–144 and B–151 each have four possible lines of symmetry.

ANSWERS:

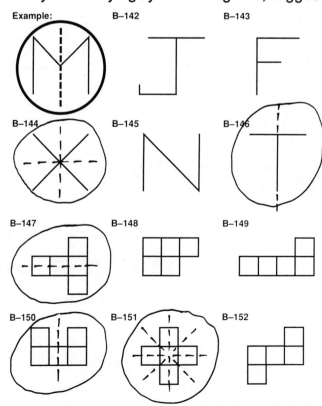

                                       P.O. BOX 448, PACIFIC GROVE, CA 93950

❑ PAGE 85: These exercises introduce the task of completing a figure using the property of symmetry. If pattern blocks are available, they may be used with the activity to picture the completed figures.

Students may also trace the given figures to complete each exercise. Ask them to suggest other strategies. (Cutting the shapes from folded paper or using a mirror are possible strategies.) How are the figures in the Example and in B–154 similar? Also, ask students whether other symmetric figures can be created using the figure in B–153.

ANSWERS:

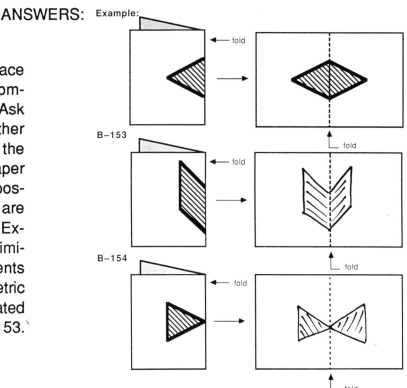

❑ PAGE 86: Letters of the alphabet are used as models of symmetry to continue the activity from page 85. Ask students to find other capital letters of the alphabet that are symmetric. Which letters have horizontal symmetry? Which have vertical? Why was the letter **E** placed on its side in B–155? Note that the **H** in B–157 has both horizontal and vertical symmetry. Which other letters of the alphabet have both?

ANSWERS:

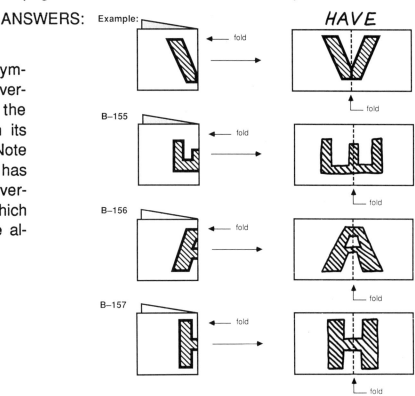

❑   PAGE 87:   These exercises are similar to those on page 84, but use the geoboard design for displaying figures. The reference points on the geoboard assist students in drawing lines of symmetry accurately. Discuss with students the types of symmetry lines (vertical, horizontal, or diagonal). Note that B–159 and B–164 have both horizontal and vertical lines of symmetry, and that B–158 has a diagonal line of symmetry. If geoboards are available the figures on this page (or different figures) can be constructed. If Figure B–162 is constructed on a geoboard, how can it be altered to create a figure with vertical symmetry?

ANSWERS:

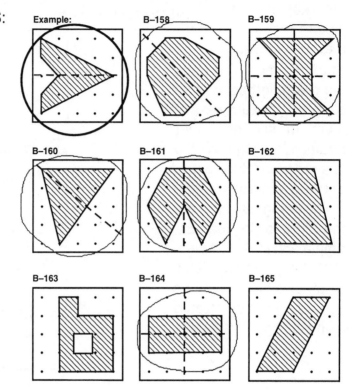

❑   PAGE 88:   This activity is similar to the activities on pages 85 and 86. Again, the geoboard design assists students in drawing accurate figures. After students have completed the exercises, ask them which figures have other lines of symmetry. The Example, B–168, B–170, and B–172 have four lines of symmetry. B–171 and B–173 have two lines of symmetry.

ANSWERS:

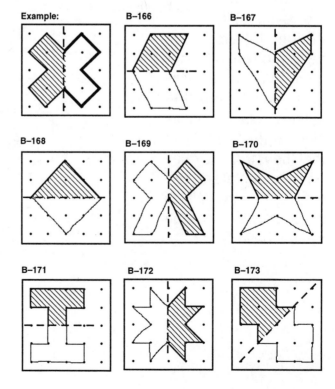

PAGES 89–94   GEOMETRIC MOTIONS

Mathematical Concepts
- Geometric motions (slides, flips, and turns)
- Congruence
- Classification using the attribute of position
- Problem-solving strategies
- Classification using the attribute of motion

VERBAL ANALYSIS STRATEGIES AND ANSWERS

❑   PAGE 89: A series of activities involving the geometric motions begin here. Encourage students to demonstrate the motion of a slide on a figure, and to verbalize the effect of the slide using manipulatives or paper cutouts of geometric shapes. How does the figure look after a slide? (It is the same shape and faces in the same direction.) Note that these activities use only horizontal slides. After completing the exercises, ask students why the other two figures in each exercise were not selected. ("They face in the wrong direction," etc., will suffice here.) Note that *turns* and *flips* of figures are discussed in the activities which follow.

ANSWERS:

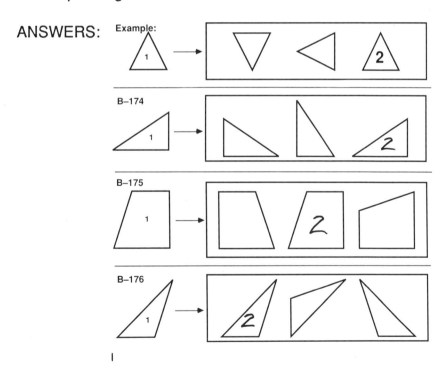

❑   PAGE 90: This page asks students to visualize a slide and to draw a matching figure after the slide. The geoboard design assists students in constructing these figures. If available, geoboards may be used to picture the figure *before* and *after* the slide. Discuss the strategy of moving each vertex of a figure "two dots to the right," then connecting these points to draw the figure after the slide. On which figures could a vertical slide be used? What would these figures look like after a vertical slide? Note that B–177 cannot be moved vertically on the geoboard.

ANSWERS:

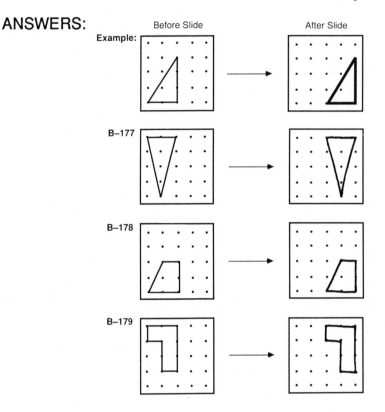

☐ PAGE 91: A second motion, *the flip*, is introduced. Again, have students explore this motion using manipulatives and verbalize their findings. How does the figure look after it has been flipped? (It is the same shape and faces in the opposite direction.) After completing the exercises, ask students to explain why the other two figures in each exercise were not selected. In the Example, the second figure in the box is in the wrong position, and the third figure represents a slide.

ANSWERS:

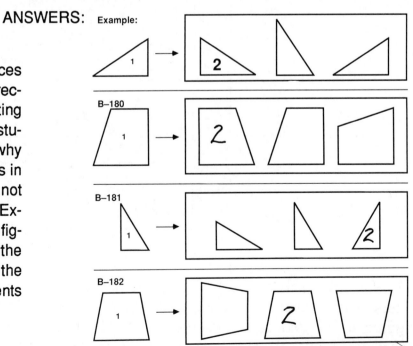

❑ PAGE 92: These activities use the geoboard design to draw a matching figure after a flip. The reference points on the geoboard assist students in constructing the matching figures. Discuss the Example with the students. If the figure in the solution were slid one dot to the left, would it still represent a flip? (Yes.) Then note that there are three possible locations for B–183 and B–184. Flips may be verified or identified by folding a page and matching the figures before and after the flip. Discuss with students the relationship between the flip motion and symmetry.

ANSWERS:

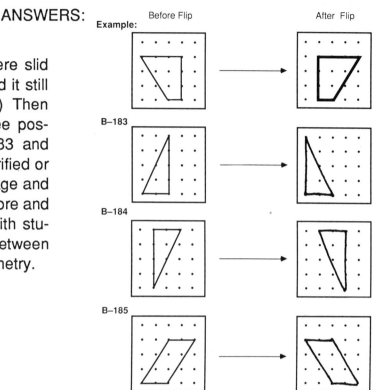

❑ PAGE 93: The third geometric motion, *the turn*, is introduced. Use manipulatives to examine and describe this motion. Although a figure can be turned any number of degrees, all turns pictured on this page are 90° clockwise (one quarter turn to the right). In the Example, B–186, and B–187, ask the students to describe the figures **not** selected in terms of the other motions. Note that the first figure in B–188 could be a slide or a flip, and the second figure could be a 180° turn or a flip across a horizontal line.

ANSWERS:

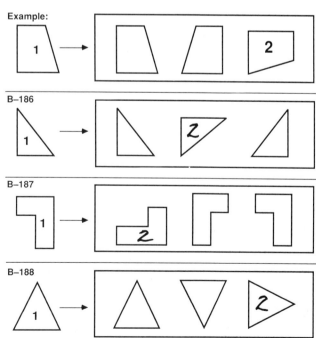

❑　PAGE 94: The geoboard design is used to assist students in drawing a matching figure after a turn. The Example suggests a 90° clockwise turn, and the other exercises should use the same turn. The earlier strategy (page 90) of transferring individual vertices may be used. Also, discuss with students the possible locations of turned figures on the geoboards, as was done for flips on page 92.

ANSWERS:

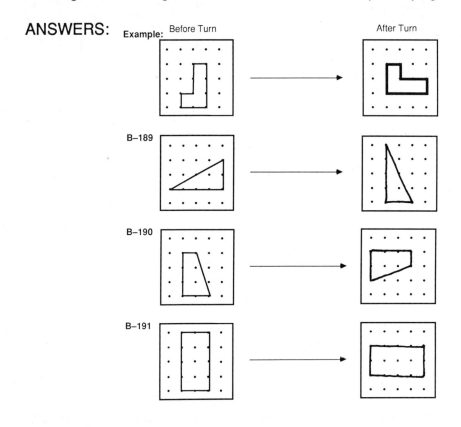

PAGES 95–100　CONGRUENT FIGURES

Mathematical Concepts
- Congruence
- Geometric motions (slides, flips, and turns)
- Similarities and differences
- Classification using geometric properties
- Strategies for comparing congruent figures
- Strategies for constructing congruent figures

VERBAL ANALYSIS STRATEGIES AND ANSWERS

❑　PAGE 95: The exercises on this page introduce the concept of congruence of geometric figures. Using the Example, discuss with students similarities and differences between the figures with respect to the number of sides, types of angles, length of sides, and parallelism. Also discuss the concept of congruence in terms of motion (that is, one figure should fit exactly on top of the other), and the strategies of using cut-out shapes, or tracing the given figure to match congruent figures. Note in the Example that response a. is the correct height but too narrow, and response d. is the correct width but too short. After the exercises are completed, ask students what geometric motion could be used to verify their answers (slides).

ANSWERS: Circle the following figures: **B–192** [d]   **B–194** [b]
B–193 [c]

❑   PAGE 96: More complex shapes are used to continue the activity from page 95. The solutions again appear in the same position, so slides can be used to verify responses. Discuss similarities and differences between figures in each exercise. Ask students to explain why the three figures not chosen are not congruent to the given figure. Review the strategies of tracing the given figure or using cutouts.

ANSWERS: Circle the following figures: **B–195** [d]   **B–197** [a]
B–196 [b]

❑   PAGE 97: The tasks from pages 95 and 96 are extended to include the geometric motion, the flip. The geoboard design allows students to make exact comparisons of the lengths of sides and reduces the need for tracing or using cutouts. Discuss with students the strategy of determining congruence by comparing the lengths of sides using the units on the geoboard. Also, stress the relative positions of the figures in the exercises. In the Example, the first choice is too small and has not been flipped.

ANSWERS:

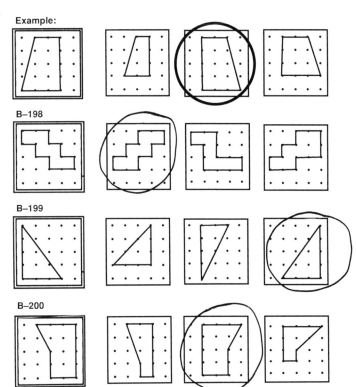

Example:

B–198

B–199

B–200

P.O. BOX 448, PACIFIC GROVE, CA 93950

❏ PAGE 98: The turn motion is used in these exercises which are similar to those on page 97. Discuss the strategy of comparing lengths and review the geometric motions. ANSWERS: Ask students to identify the common properties of all the figures in each exercise. (In B–201 all figures are right triangles.) Also, ask students to explain why the other two figures in each exercise were not chosen.

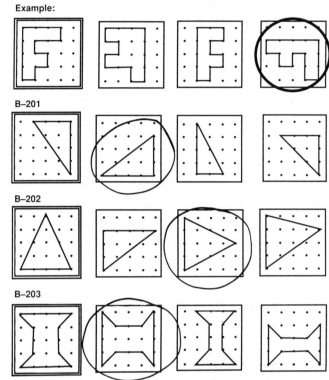

❏ PAGE 99: These exercises require the construction of figures congruent to a given figure. Again, the geoboard design aids in producing accurate figures. Note that although no mention is made of geometric motions, the solution to the Example suggests a slide. Discuss what this solution might look like if it were flipped or turned. Also discuss the strategy from page 90 of transferring each vertex independently to the blank geoboard and then connecting points. Note that there is more than one solution to each exercise, since figures could appear in several locations by slides, flips, or turns.

POSSIBLE ANSWERS:

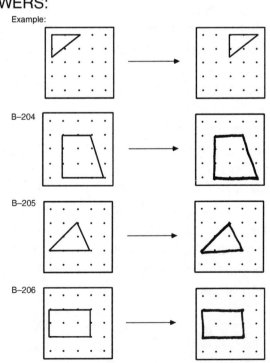

❑ PAGE 100: This page introduces more complex figures to continue the pre-vious activity. Review with students the strategy from page 99. If vertices are transferred to the blank geoboard, discuss the importance of order when connect-ing points. In B–207 there is only one way to connect the three points. This is not true in B–208 or B–209. As on page 99, there are multiple solutions. What would the solutions look like if slides, flips, or turns were used?

ANSWERS:

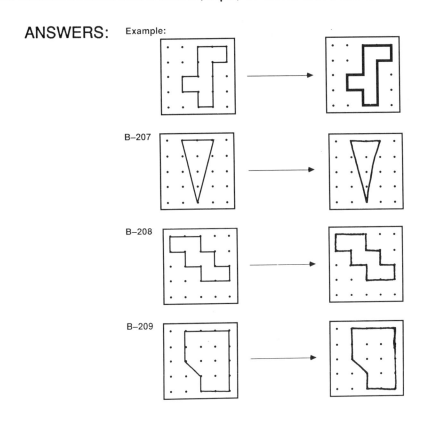

PAGES 101–104   SIMILAR FIGURES

Mathematical Concepts
- Similarity of geometric figures
- Similarities and differences
- Enlargement and reduction of figures
- Congruence of angles

VERBAL ANALYSIS STRATEGIES AND ANSWERS

❑ PAGE 101: The concept of similarity is introduced in these exercises. Note that while congruent figures are similar to one another, on this page all similar figures are either larger or smaller than the given figure. This strategy emphasizes that similar figures need not be the same size. Discuss two properties of similar figures: 1) matching angles must be the same size, and 2) one figure must be a reduction or an enlargement of the other figure. In the Example, choices a., b., and d. can be eliminated by comparing angles. In c., the three angles match those of the given figure. Also note that c. is smaller and a reduction of the given triangle. In B–210, c. can be eliminated by comparing angles, and a. and b. eliminated because they are not reductions of the given square (even though all angles are right angles).

ANSWERS: Circle the following figures: **B–210** [d]   **B–212** [b]
                                                        B–211 [b]

❏ PAGE 102: More complex figures are introduced in this activity. Note that in the Example, B–214, and B–215 all of the angles match, and the selection of a similar figure involves the concept of reduction/enlargement. Also, note that each solution on the page is an enlargement of the given figure.

ANSWERS: Circle the following figures: **B–213** [d]   **B–215** [a]
                                                        B–214 [c]

❏ PAGE 103: These exercises require the construction of figures similar to but *smaller than* a given figure. As before, the geoboard design aids in producing accurate figures. The solution to the Example suggests a one-half reduction and a slide. Reductions other than one-half are possible, but require the use of one-half units on the geoboard (in the Example, a horizontal side of one-half and a vertical side of one unit). Note that in B–217, to reduce this figure by one-half, students must use one-half units on the geoboard (see the solution). Discuss other possible solutions by sliding, flipping, or turning the figures in the solutions.

ANSWERS:

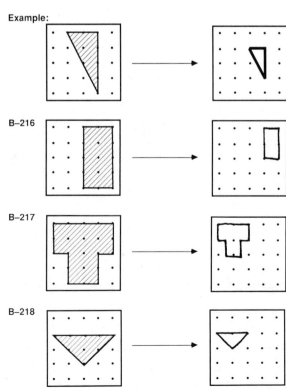

❑ PAGE 104: This activity is similar to that on page 103. However, the solutions are *enlargements* of the given figures. The solution to the Example suggests a slide and a doubling of the sides of the given figure. Again, discuss alternate solutions by sliding, flipping, or turning the figures in the solutions.

ANSWERS:

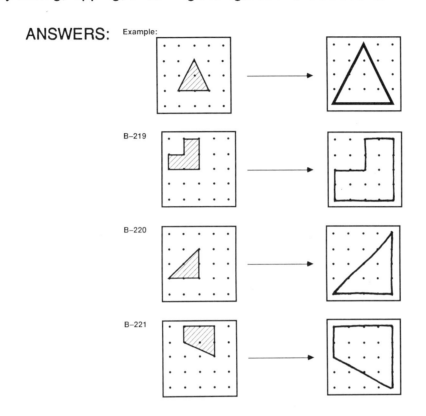

PAGES 105–110 COMBINING SHAPES

Mathematical Concepts
- Congruence
- Geometric motions (slides, flips, and turns)
- Strategies for comparing congruent figures
- Strategies for constructing congruent figures
- Combining regions

VERBAL ANALYSIS STRATEGIES AND ANSWERS

❑ PAGE 105: The task of identifying regions that can be constructed by combining two simpler shapes is introduced one this page. Stress that both given shapes (the square and the rectangle) must be used. How are B–222 and B–223 similar? What shapes would be needed to construct these regions? (Two rectangles.) What figure would result if two squares were combined? Ask students to compare B–222 and B–224. How are they similar and how are they different? Ask students to investigate other possible figures (besides the Example and B–224) that can be formed. If available, attribute blocks (INVICTA desk set size) may be used in conjunction with this activity.

ANSWERS: Put an X on: **B–224**

❏   PAGE 106: Two different shapes are used to continue the activity from page 105. These shapes are based on pattern blocks. Stress that both given shapes must be used. If pattern blocks are available, ask students which combinations of blocks could be used to construct B–225 and B–226. As before, ask students to find other figures which can be formed using the two given shapes. What figures can be formed using two trapezoids or two triangles? What figures can be formed using three triangles?

ANSWERS: Put an X on: **B–227**

❏   PAGE 107: These exercises continue the task of identifying regions formed by two given shapes. Use the geoboard design to assist students in identifying shapes congruent to the given shapes. Discuss the strategy of locating shapes in the figures that are congruent to the given shapes. Remind students that shapes may be slid, flipped, or turned. In the Example, the given trapezoid has been slid up one unit, and the given triangle has been turned or flipped before joining it to the trapezoid. Ask students to verbalize the geometric motions illustrated in the solutions (B–229 and B–230), and encourage them to verbalize why B–232 is not a solution. (The trapezoids are congruent, but the triangles are not.) If two of the given trapezoids were used, could the figures pictured in B–228 and B–231 be covered? (Yes.)

ANSWERS: Put an X on: **B–229   B–230**

❏   PAGE 108: Three given shapes are used in these exercises to extend the previous activity. Discuss the strategy from page 107, again stressing geometric motions. Ask students to analyze the solutions in terms of geometric motions, and have them explain why B–236 and B–237 are not solutions. Students should then compare the two solutions B–233 and B–235. How are they related? (One is a rotation of the other.)

ANSWERS: Put an X on: **B–233   B–234   B–235**

❑ PAGE 109: On this page students are asked to construct their own regions by combining two given shapes. The geoboard design will assist in constructing triangles congruent to the given triangles. Encourage students to make figures that are not merely slides, rotations, or flips of other figures they make. If necessary, suggest they use triangular cutouts to discover possible solutions. After students complete the exercises, ask them to consider turns or flips of their solutions. Discuss the number of unique solutions that were drawn.

ANSWERS:

Example: 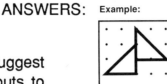 B–238 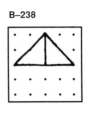 B–239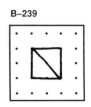

B–240 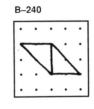 B–241 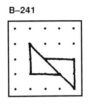 B–242

❑ PAGE 110: This extends the previous activity by using three given shapes. Students may again need to use cutouts or tracing to discover possible solutions. Review the solutions in terms of geometric motions. Six unique solutions are pictured here. After students complete the exercises, determine if other solutions were found.

ANSWERS:

Example: 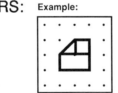 B–243 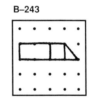 B–244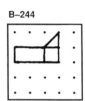

B–245 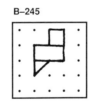 B–246 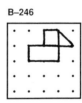 B–247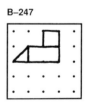

PAGES 111–114 MATCHING AND FINDING SHAPES

Mathematical Concepts
- Comparing congruent figures
- Combining figures
- Strategies for comparing regions
- Geometric motions

VERBAL ANALYSIS STRATEGIES AND ANSWERS

❑ PAGE 111: The task illustrated on this page is to construct a square region by combining two parts. Discuss with students three possible strategies for analyzing the figures: 1) consider the *whole* square and match it with a square that is identical except for shading; 2) consider only the *shaded* part of a square (in the Example, a right triangle) and match it with a congruent unshaded figure (the white right triangle in the Example); and 3) sliding the shaded part of each figure in the exercises to the appropriate square in the right column so that the square is completely shaded.

ANSWERS: Example:

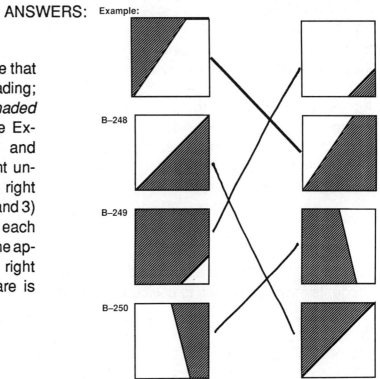

❑ PAGE 112: These exercises continue those on the previous page but use circular regions. The center of each circle is shown for reference. Discuss the strategies from page 111. In the Example, the missing part must meet the center of the circle. Discuss the two possible choices from the right column. Why is the second figure from the top not a solution? Discuss with the students the role of the center of the circle in B–251 and B–253 in determining the solution.

ANSWERS: Example:

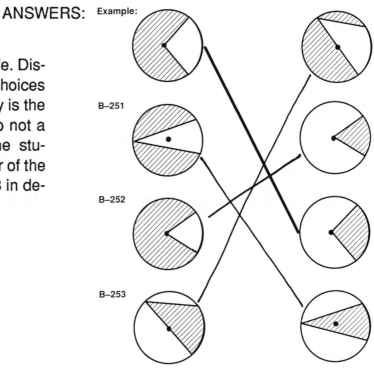

❑ PAGE 113: This page introduces the task of locating congruent shapes embedded in a more complex figure. Note that the shapes used in the complex figures do not overlap. However, in the Example, solution a. could be identified by matching it to either the lower rectangle in the figure or to the upper rectangle (which has a diagonal drawn). Also, solution d. could be identified by matching it to either the upper triangle (this requires a turn) or to the lower triangle (with a slide). Discuss solutions in terms of congruence and motions. For example, solutions a. and b. in B–256 require slides, but solution c. requires a turn.

ANSWERS: Put an X on the following shapes: **B–254** [b, d]
B–255 [c, d]
B–256 [a, b, c]

❑ PAGE 114: More complex shapes are used in these exercises to continue the activity from page 113. In terms of geometric motions, only slides are used. After completing and discussing the exercises, pose the following question: "In each exercise, if the interior subdivision lines are disregarded, would the two shapes not selected fit into the given region?" (Yes.)

ANSWERS: Put an X on the following shapes: **B–257** [a, b]
B–258 [c, d]
B–259 [c, d]

PAGES 115–116 DIVIDING FIGURES

Mathematical Concepts
• Dividing a region into parts
• Decomposition
• Comparing decompositions of a region
• Describing decompositions

VERBAL ANALYSIS STRATEGIES AND ANSWERS

❑ PAGE 115: This page introduces the concept of decomposition (subdivision) of a region into parts (squares and triangles). Observe that the solutions pictured here are not unique. After students complete the exercises, ask them to compare their subdivisions to the solutions of other students. Note that in the solution to the Example, squares can be subdivided into two triangles. Also note that the solution shown for B–260 leaves points in the interior of the squares. Could this be done with any other figures? (Yes, in the Example and in B–265.)

ANSWERS: Example:

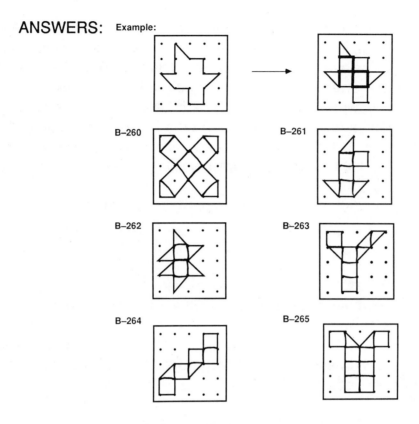

B–260   B–261

B–262   B–263

B–264   B–265

☐   PAGE 116: The activity from the previous page is continued using figures with more interior points. The solutions pictured here are not unique. Again, ask students to compare their solutions in terms of the shapes used and the number of subdivisions. Ask students if, when considering their solutions, they could have used larger subdivisions or smaller subdivisions (squares or triangles with and without interior points).

ANSWERS: Example: B–266

B–267   B–268

B–269   B–270

B–271   B–272

INTRODUCTION TO OPERATIONS

The **Operations** section of **MATHEMATICAL REASONING** builds upon the **Number and Numeration** section and offers students an opportunity to investigate and discuss the arithmetic operations as they apply to whole numbers. The use of formal language and the properties of these operations are included in a later section (**Relations**).

This section addresses two major themes:

- the conceptual development of three of the arithmetic operations (+, x, −)
- the application of these operations in computation and problem solving

Activities that ask students to analyze and describe the composition and decomposition of sets are used to build an understanding of the operation of addition. Activities that incorporate a monetary model are also used to reinforce the relationship of composition and decomposition of sets to the operation of addition.

The operation of subtraction is approached by using missing addends, while the operation of multiplication is introduced by the use of arrays. The groundwork for division is laid through a series of exercises involving missing factors.

The activities in this section relating to computation and problem solving assume that students have a knowledge of the basic arithmetic facts. Computational activities include:

INTRODUCTION TO
OPERATIONS
(continued)

- identifying equal sums, products, and differences
- using inequalities to compare computations
- construction of elementary number sentences
- developing strategies for use in computation and comparison

The problem-solving activities ask students to analyze word problems and to select the appropriate operations needed to determine the solutions to these problems. The use of rounding and estimating as a mathematical tool is also introduced in conjunction with the operations of addition and multiplication.

PAGES 117–122   COUNTING TO TEN

Mathematical Concepts
• Union of sets
• Cardinality of sets
• Number decomposition
• Grouping elements in a set (2–10)
• Strategies used in decomposition
• Constructing models for decomposition
• Comparing decompositions

VERBAL ANALYSIS STRATEGIES AND ANSWERS

❑   PAGE 117: These exercises begin a series dealing with the decomposition of a number. This page considers combinations that are equal to five. Discuss two strategies for these exercises: 1) start with the given set of dots and use *counting on* with each possible set in the right column; and 2) compare the given set to a set of five to determine how many dots are needed to complete a set of five, then locate the correct set in the right column. Using the first strategy, ask students to explain why the first two sets in the right column do not match the Example. (Pairing the first set with the Example would make a set of seven; pairing the second set with the Example would make a set of eight.) It is also possible to use manipulatives to form sets of five and have students decompose the sets to correspond to each exercise on the page.

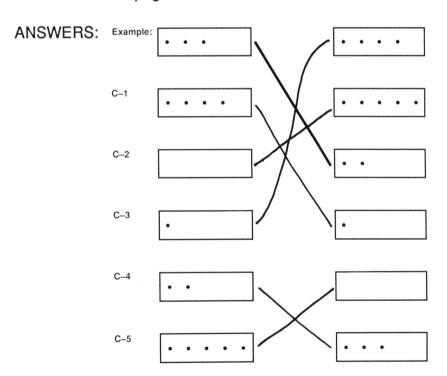

ANSWERS:

❑ PAGE 118: In this activity sets of six are used to continue the concept of decomposition. Discuss the two strategies used on page 117. After the exercises are completed, ask students to compare the following pairs of exercises: C–6 and C–9, C–7 and C–11. Also, ask the students if there is another exercise that could be paired with C–10. (Yes, a set of zero dots with a set of six dots.) Is the same true for C–8? (No, there would still be two sets of three dots each.) Again, manipulatives can be used as suggested on page 117.

ANSWERS:

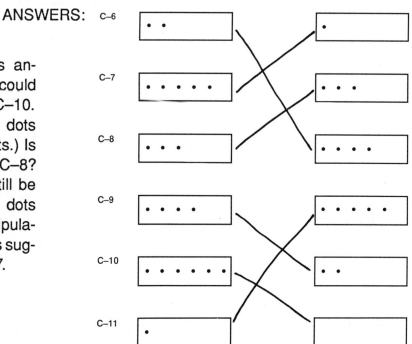

❑ PAGE 119: Sets of nine are used to further explore decomposition. Continue using the earlier strategies discussed on page 117. Upon completion of the exercises, ask students to compare C–13 and C–17 (the decomposition of 9 into 3, 6 and into 6, 3). For each of the remaining exercises, ask students to explain the reverse decomposition. For example, C–12 represents a 5, 4 decomposition of 9, so the reverse would be a 4, 5 decomposition. Consider using manipulatives to construct and explain these decompositions.

ANSWERS:

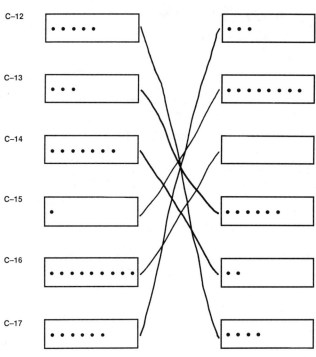

❑   PAGE 120: These exercises use sets of ten in decomposition. After completing the exercises, have students explain the relationship between exercises C–20 and C–23. Also, have students construct the reverse decomposition for the other exercises as explained on page 119. Note that C–19 has only one decomposition (reversing a 5, 5 decomposition is still a 5, 5 decomposition).

ANSWERS: C–18

C–19

C–20

C–21

C–22

C–23

❑   PAGE 121: Exploration of the decomposition of sets is continued using rectangular arrays. The exercises emphasize counting and entering data into a table. After students complete the tables, discuss the solutions in terms of the numbers 2, 3, or 4. For example, in C–25 the second row in the table is a 2,1 decomposition of a set of three squares, and the third row—1, 2—is the reverse decomposition. Also, in C–25 the top and bottom rows in the table are reverse decompositions. Using manipulatives (cubes or tiles) to construct the arrays would enable students to physically separate the sets to correspond to the decompositions in the solutions.

ANSWERS:

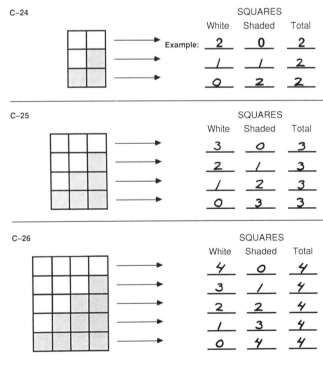

C–24

SQUARES		
White	Shaded	Total
Example: 2	0	2
1	1	2
0	2	2

C–25

SQUARES		
White	Shaded	Total
3	0	3
2	1	3
1	2	3
0	3	3

C–26

SQUARES		
White	Shaded	Total
4	0	4
3	1	4
2	2	4
1	3	4
0	4	4

P.O. BOX 448, PACIFIC GROVE, CA 93950

❏   PAGE 122: This page concludes the series on decomposition. Rectangular arrays are used again to decompose sets of five and six. After students complete the exercises, explore the various decomposition relationships of the rows in each table. Using manipulatives will allow students to physically decompose sets of five and six into all the possible decompositions listed in the tables. Encourage them to describe the decompositions in terms of white squares versus shaded squares.

ANSWERS: C–27

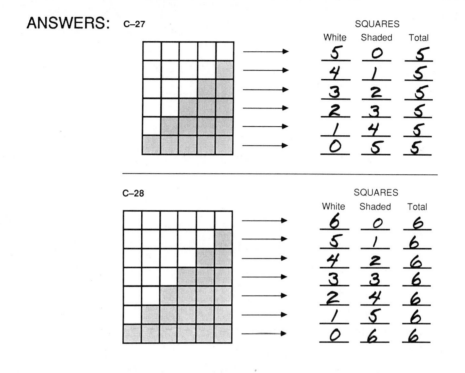

C–27 table:

White	Shaded	Total
5	0	5
4	1	5
3	2	5
2	3	5
1	4	5
0	5	5

C–28 table (SQUARES):

White	Shaded	Total
6	0	6
5	1	6
4	2	6
3	3	6
2	4	6
1	5	6
0	6	6

PAGES 123–126   SUMS USING COINS

Mathematical Concepts
• Decomposition
• Matching sets
• Grouping by 5, 10, and 25
• Applications of decomposition
• Constructing sets with a given cardinal number
• Counting in multiples (5, 10, and 25)

VERBAL ANALYSIS STRATEGIES AND ANSWERS

❏   PAGE 123: Coins are used in this activity to introduce an application of decomposition. Discuss with students the relationships between the penny, nickel, and dime. Prior to working these activities, have students decompose a dime into two sets using combinations of nickels and pennies (there are only three possible decompositions). Two strategies can be discussed for completing the exercises: 1) comparing each given set to the three possible decompositions mentioned above, or 2) counting (pennies in C–32 and C–33) and counting on (from five) in the remaining exercises. Note that C–29 and C–33 represent decompositions of nine. Is there any other combination of nickels and pennies that decomposes nine? (No.) In the uncircled sets, how many pennies would have to be added to each set to equal a dime?

ANSWERS: Circle the following exercises: **C–31**   **C–32**

❑   PAGE 124: This page extends the activity from page 123 by using a quarter instead of a dime. Discuss with students the relationships between the quarter, dime, nickel, and penny. Prior to working the exercises, discuss the decomposition of a quarter into pennies, nickels, and dimes. (There are many decompositions; however, there are only three combinations using nickels and dimes.) Students can use the first strategy from page 123 to compare these models to the exercises containing only nickels and dimes. In the exercises with pennies (C–37 and C–38), students can use a strategy of counting in multiples together with counting on. In C–38, a student may say "10, 20, 21, 22, 23, 24, 25." In the uncircled exercises, ask students what coin combinations could be added to make each set equal a quarter. (There are two possible combinations for each.)

ANSWERS: Circle the following exercises: **C–34**   **C–38**
                                                   C–36   **C–39**

❑   PAGE 125: Students are asked to construct a set of coins equal to a given number. Two mathematical processes are used in the exercises: 1) counting using multiples, then counting on, and 2) determining a decomposition of a given number. In the Example, ask students to count the selected nickels with multiple counting (5, 10, 15), and to proceed with counting on for the selected pennies (16, 17, 18). Ask if there is a different solution to the Example. (Yes—5, 10, 11; 12,... 18.) Note that each exercise has at least two different solutions. After completing the exercises, ask students to compare solutions and discuss how many are possible for each exercise.

ANSWERS:

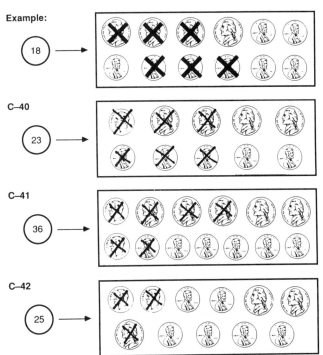

❑   PAGE 126: These exercises extend the task from page 125 by introducing the quarter to some sets. Review the strategy from page 125 of counting in multiples and counting on. Note that C–43 and C–44 do not have unique solutions. Ask students to compare solutions and to determine the possible decompositions using the coins in the given sets. Note that C–45 and C–46 have unique solutions. In C–45 and C–46, ask students whether the replacement of a dime with two nickels in the set would create alternative solutions. (Yes.)

ANSWERS:

C–43   47 →

C–44   62 →

C–45   80 →

C–46   56 →

PAGES 127–130   SUMS TO TEN

Mathematical Concepts
- Decomposition of a set
- Operation of addition
- Addition facts (5–10)
- Comparing decompositions
- Constructing models for decompositions and addition
- Commutativity of addition

VERBAL ANALYSIS STRATEGIES AND ANSWERS

❑   PAGE 127: The relationship between the decomposition of a set of five and the addition facts associated with five is introduced here. (This activity assumes student knowledge of the addition facts for five in order to fill in the "sum" column.) As in earlier exercises, students are asked to identify a decomposition and record data in a table. After completing the exercises, ask students to describe the data in the table in two ways: 1) as a set decomposition (the Example shows a 4, 1 decomposition of the set of circles); and 2) as a sum of two numbers—"4 white circles plus 1 black circle equals 5 circles." Again ask students to identify reverse decompositions (for example, C–47 and C–50) and relate them to reverse sums (commutativity of addition).

ANSWERS: **C–47** [2 + 3 = 5]   **C–49** [1 + 4 = 5]   **C–51** [0 + 5 = 5]
               C–48 [5 + 0 = 5]   **C–50** [3 + 2 = 5]

❑   PAGE 128: This activity continues the concept from page 127, using decomposition and addition facts for six. Have students verbalize their solutions in the two ways discussed on page 127. Ask students to identify reverse decompositions and relate them to reverse sums (commutativity). Note that C–53 does not have a reverse decomposition.

ANSWERS: **C–52** [2 + 4 = 6]   **C–54** [1 + 5 = 6]   **C–56** [0 + 6 = 6]
               C–53 [3 + 3 = 6]   **C–55** [4 + 2 = 6]   **C–57** [5 + 1 = 6]

❑   PAGE 129: The reverse mathematical process to that used on pages 127 and 128 is introduced in these exercises. Given a number sentence, students are asked to interpret this sum as a decomposition and construct a decomposition model. Note in the Example that the two white circles appear to the left in the set, and the four black circles to the right. Suggest that students follow this format when doing the exercises. Ask students if there are any reverse sums or decompositions on the page (there are none). In exercises C–58 to C–61, ask students to state the reverse sum and to describe its decomposition in terms of white and black circles.

ANSWERS:

	White Circles		Black Circles		Sum	
Example:	2	+	4	=	6	→ ○○●●●●
C–58	5	+	2	=	7	→ ○○○○○●●
C–59	4	+	3	=	7	→ ○○○○●●●
C–60	5	+	1	=	6	→ ○○○○○●
C–61	0	+	7	=	7	→ ●●●●●●●
C–62	3	+	3	=	6	→ ○○○●●●

❑ PAGE 130: This activity continues that of page 129, using sums of nine and ten. Suggest that students follow the format from the previous page when filling in circles (white on left, black on right). In each exercise, ask students to state the reverse sum and to describe its decomposition in terms of white and black circles.

ANSWERS:

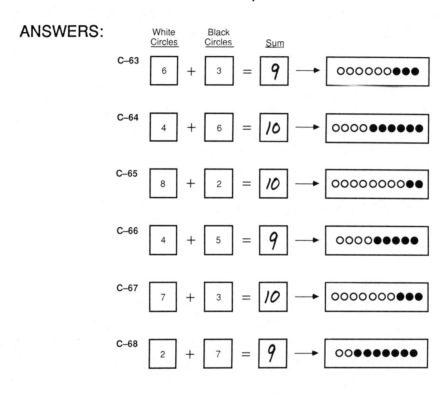

PAGES 131–132 GROUPING BY TENS

Mathematical Concepts
- Grouping by tens
- Place value
- Decomposition of sets of 10
- Decomposition of sets greater than 10

VERBAL ANALYSIS STRATEGIES AND ANSWERS

❑ PAGE 131: These exercises extend the concept of decomposition to sets containing more than ten circles and use the concept of place value to describe the decompositions. Note in the Example that circles are shaded consecutively from the left until ten are filled in. Encourage students to use this format in the exercises. Discuss with students the relationship between the numbers in the boxes and the decomposition of the sets into black and white circles. In the Example, 13 corresponds to a decomposition into ten black circles and three white circles. Also, make students aware of the decomposition of 10 by relating the black circles in the two given sets. In the Example, 10 is decomposed into 7, 3.

ANSWERS:

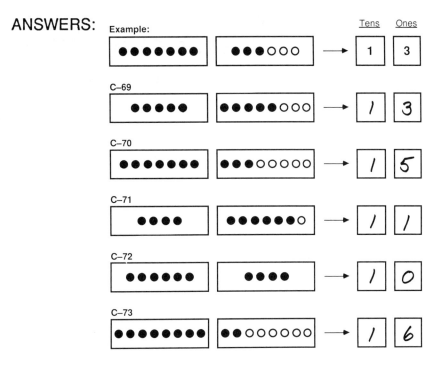

PAGE 132: The activity from page 131 is extended to sets of more than twenty circles. In each set, the groupings of the circles are not unique. Ask students to compare their groupings. Although students may have grouped the circles differently, the numbers recorded in the boxes should match. Encourage students to use the recorded numbers to verbalize the decomposition of the sets of circles. In the Example, the 26 has been decomposed into two groups of ten circles and six ungrouped circles. Manipulative materials (place-value blocks) may be used to supplement the exercises and aid in the description of the decomposition.

ANSWERS:

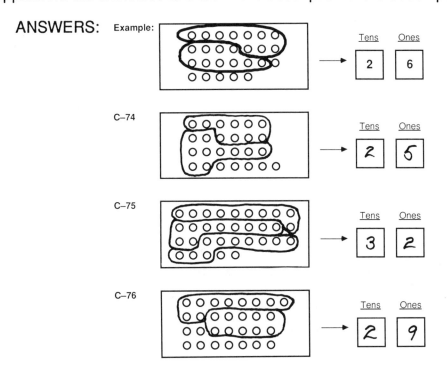

PAGES 133–138 USING BASIC FACTS (SUMS)

Mathematical Concepts
- Addition facts (sums to 20)
- Missing addends (sums of 10)
- Ordering (greater than, less than)
- Sums with three addends (sums of 10)
- Decomposition of sets
- Reverse sums (commutativity)

VERBAL ANALYSIS STRATEGIES AND ANSWERS

❑ PAGE 133: Students are asked to match addition facts to a given sum. (It is assumed in these exercises that students know their addition facts.) After completing the exercises, ask students how the two answers in the Example are related. Then ask if any other answers have the same relationship. (Yes, C–83.) Encourage students to explain the circled facts in terms of decompositions of a set. In each exercise, ask students if they can find another decomposition using *two single-digit numbers.* This is possible in all exercises except C–82.

ANSWERS: **C–77** [3 + 6]   **C–81** [2 + 6, 7 + 1]
          C–78 [8 + 8, 7 + 9] **C–82** [9 + 9]
          C–79 [9 + 2, 5 + 6] **C–83** [9 + 6, 6 + 9]
          C–80 [8 + 4]

❑ PAGE 134: A knowledge of basic addition facts is used in this activity to separate a set into two subsets—sums greater than 15 and sums less than 15. Note that the only addition facts for 15 are 6 + 9, 7 + 8, and 10 + 5. After completing the activity, encourage students to compare the given facts to 6 + 9, 7 + 8, and 10 + 5. Thus, 7 + 9 belongs in set C–85 because it is one more than 7 + 8, or 15. Also 9 + 5 belongs in set C–84 because it is one less than 6 + 9, or 15. Compare these last two facts with exercises C–88 and C–89. Discuss with students that the answer to C–88 must appear in set C–84 and be the largest sum in that set. Ask students which set contains the answer to C–89. (C–85)

ANSWERS: **C–84** [3 + 5, 8 + 5, 7 + 5, 3 + 2, 4 + 5, 6 + 7, 9 + 5, 4 + 5]
          C–85 [10 + 10, 8 + 9, 9 + 9, 8 + 10, 9 + 8, 7 + 9, 10 + 9, 10 + 7]
          C–86 [Less than, circle 9 + 5; Greater than, circle 10 + 10]
          C–87 [Less than, X on 3 + 2; Greater than, X on 7 + 9]
          C–88 [9 + 5]
          C–89 [7 + 9]

❑ PAGE 135: This page introduces the concept of missing addends in basic facts whose sum is ten. After completing the exercises, ask students to compare the Example to C–97. How are they related? (They are reverse sums.) Ask students to find other pairs of exercises that are similarly related. Note that C–92 and C–94 are not reversed, and that C–93 has no reverse sum. Using manipulatives may help some students find the missing addend. In the Example, a set of ten cubes can be decomposed into a set of nine and a set of one (the missing addend).

ANSWERS: **C–90** [8]   **C–92** [6]   **C–94** [4]   **C–96** [2]
     C–91 [7]   **C–93** [5]   **C–95** [3]   **C–97** [9]

❑ PAGE 136: The activity on page 135 is extended here to sums with three addends. The strategy for solving these exercises is a two-step process: 1) sum the two known addends, and 2) use that sum to determine the missing addend needed to make ten. After completing the exercises, ask students to compare C–98 and C–104. (They have the same addends in different orders.) Are there any other pairs of exercises related similarly? Ask students to find other sets of three addends with a sum of ten that are different from the exercises (e.g., 3 + 3 + 4). Manipulatives may be used to decompose ten into three sets to find the missing addends.

ANSWERS: **C–98** [2]   **C–101** [7]   **C–104** [6]
     C–99 [0]   **C–102** [0]   **C–105** [4]
     C–100 [3]   **C–103** [1]   **C–106** [8]

❑ PAGE 137: These exercises are based on addition facts whose sums are ten, and relates them to missing addends. Prior to beginning the exercises, discuss the addition facts whose sums are ten (1 + 9, 2 + 8, 3 + 7, 4 + 6, 5 + 5, and their reverse sums). Discuss two strategies for solving the Example: 1) search the row for a pair of numbers that matches one of the addition facts listed above (only one pair is found— 8, 2); or 2) start with 5 and look for the missing addend in the row to make 10 (not there), then try 8 and repeat the procedure. (Here we find the missing addend, 2).

ANSWERS: **C–107** [5, 5]   **C–110** [4, 6]   **C–112** [2, 8]
     C–108 [3, 7]   **C–111** [7, 3]   **C–113** [4, 6]
     C–109 [1, 9]

❑ PAGE 138: Page 137 is extended in this activity by including three addends that sum to ten. Using the Example, discuss with students the following strategy. First use the given number (6) to find the missing addend needed to make a sum of ten (4). Then search the row for a pair of numbers whose sum is four (3 and 1).

Discuss the use of the two strategies from page 137 to find this pair of numbers. In C–117 some students may circle 5 to make a sum of ten. Remind students that two numbers must be circled, so the answer is 4 and 1. The same is true in C–119 and C–120.

ANSWERS: **C–114** [5, 1]   **C–117** [4, 1]   **C–119** [2, 2]
              C–115 [2, 1]   **C–118** [3, 5; 2, 6]   **C–120** [1, 1]
              C–116 [4, 3]

PAGES 139–142   EQUAL LENGTHS AND REGIONS

Mathematical Concepts
- Missing addends
- Geometric model for missing addends
- Decomposition of lengths
- One-to-one matching
- Recording data in a table
- Interpreting data in a table
- Comparing regions

VERBAL ANALYSIS STRATEGIES AND ANSWERS

❑   PAGE 139: These exercises introduce a geometric model for missing addends. In the Example, point out to students that the left edges of figures A and B are aligned, making comparison easier.

Also, discuss two strategies for solving the problem: 1) How many squares must be added to A to make B; and 2) decompose B into length A and another length of two squares. Both of these strategies determine the missing addend, 2.

ANSWERS:

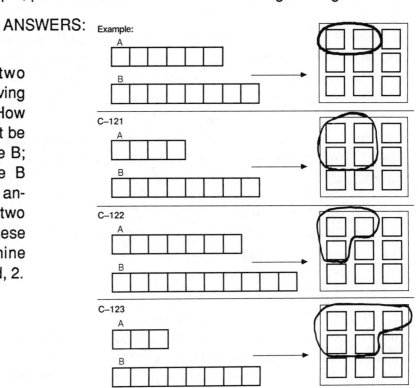

❑ PAGE 140: The activity from page 139 is extended on this page with figures whose endpoints are not aligned. Discuss the need for developing a new strategy to solve the exercises. One such strategy would be pairing squares in A with those in B. In Exercise C–124 there are four squares in length A. Place X's on four squares in length B. The remaining squares in B indicate how many must be added to A to make a length of B. Alternatively, students could draw lines between pairs of matched squares in A and B. Then the number of squares in B not paired with A determine the solution.

ANSWERS:

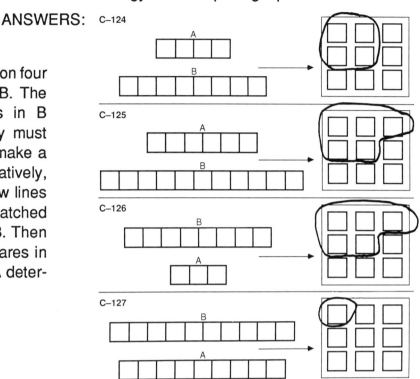

❑ PAGE 141: This page extends the activity from page 140 by asking students to record data in a table. Since students must record the number of squares in each length, the strategy of putting X's on squares in B is the better method for these exercises. After completing the exercises, encourage students to use the data to verbalize the geometric model. In the Example 8, 5, 3 means: length B has eight squares, length A has five squares, so three squares are needed to make length A equal to length B.

ANSWERS: **C–128** [7, 6, 1]   **C–129** [10, 7, 3]   **C–130** [8, 4, 4]

❑ PAGE 142: The concepts on page 141 are extended in these exercises with rectangular regions replacing lengths. For the initial activity of counting squares, discuss earlier strategies of counting using multiples (2, 3, 4, 5). Again, the strategy of placing X's on squares in figure B can be used to determine the "Number Needed" in the table. Rather than putting X's on individual squares in B, discuss with students the strategy of locating all of figure A within figure B and shading that part of B. Then the number of unshaded squares in B is the "Number Needed" in the table.

ANSWERS: **C–131** [15, 5, 10]   **C–132** [12, 6, 6]   **C–133** [20, 8, 12]

PAGES 143–148 MISSING ADDENDS/DIFFERENCES

Mathematical Concepts
- Missing addends
- Replacement set
- Multiple solutions to a number sentence
- Subtraction operation
- Open sentences involving subtraction

VERBAL ANALYSIS STRATEGIES AND ANSWERS

❏ PAGE 143: These exercises extend the task of finding missing addends to sums greater than ten. In the Example and exercises C–134 to C–137, only one addend is missing and the solutions are unique. Students may use previous strategies to find the missing addends or use trial and error with the given set of numbers (replacement set). In C–138 to C–140 the two addends are missing. Stress that students must select their pair of addends from the replacement set. For example, in C–138 students cannot use 10 + 5 because these are not in the given set. Since the solutions to the last three exercises are not unique, ask students to compare their solutions to determine if all possible solutions have been found.

ANSWERS: **C–134** [4]   **C–138** [6, 9   8, 7   4, 11   12, 3]
          C–135 [8]   **C–139** [6, 7   8, 5   4, 9]
          C–136 [4]   **C–140** [5, 6   8, 3   4, 7]
          C–137 [5]

❏ PAGE 144: The task of finding missing addends which are unique is continued. These exercises are similar to those on page 135, but include sums other than ten. Manipulatives may be used as suggested on page 135.

ANSWERS: **C–141** [6]   **C–144** [2]   **C–147** [5]
          C–142 [5]   **C–145** [8]   **C–148** [9]
          C–143 [3]   **C–146** [4]

❏ PAGE 145: This page introduces the arithmetic operation of subtraction. A replacement set is once again used to aid in solving the exercises. In the Example, discuss possible strategies such as: 1) trial and error using numbers from the replacement set, or 2) the missing addend relationship, "What number must be added to 4 to get a sum of 11?" As before, note that solutions to the Example and C–149 through C–153 are unique. In the last two exercises, two numbers are missing and the solutions are not unique. However, solutions must come from the replacement set. Ask students to compare solutions to determine if all possible ones have been found.

           P.O. BOX 448, PACIFIC GROVE, CA 93950

ANSWERS: **C–149** [15]   **C–153** [6]
          C–150 [8]   **C–154** [7, 4   10, 7   11, 8   13, 10]
          C–151 [15]   **C–155** [15, 10   13, 8   11, 6]
          C–152 [13]

❑ PAGE 146: The task of completing open sentences involving subtraction continues in this activity. The solutions in each exercise are unique. Emphasize the relationship between subtraction and missing addends discussed on page 145. Discuss the difference between solving the Example and solving C–157. In the Example students are asked, "What number must be added to 7 to get a sum of 15?" In C–157 students are asked, "The number 6 added to 4 gives what sum?"

ANSWERS: **C–156** [7]   **C–159** [10]   **C–162** [5]
          C–157 [10]   **C–160** [9]   **C–163** [16]
          C–158 [17]   **C–161** [10]

❑ PAGE 147: These exercises are similar to those on page 133, but with sums replaced by differences. (It is assumed that students can perform simple subtraction related to number facts.) After completing the exercises, ask students to express each circled solution in terms of missing addends. In the Example, 6 + 6 = 12 and 6 + 5 = 11.

ANSWERS: **C–164** [12 – 7]   **C–168** [14 – 9]
          C–165 [12 – 4, 16 – 8]   **C–169** [15 – 9, 12 – 6]
          C–166 [12 – 9, 7 – 4]   **C–170** [13 – 9]
          C–167 [15 – 8]

❑ PAGE 148: A knowledge of basic subtraction related to number facts is used on this page to separate a set into two subsets—differences less than 10 and differences greater than 10. Discuss with students where the answers to C–175 and C–176 can be found (in set C–171 and set C–172). Note that the circled value in C–171 is the solution to C–175, and the crossed-out value in C–172 is the solution to C–176.

ANSWERS: **C–171** [15 – 7, 18 – 9, 13 – 5, 13 – 7, 14 – 9,
                16 – 9, 14 – 7, 12 – 5]
          C–172 [16 – 3, 17 – 3, 18 – 6, 17 – 6, 16 – 2,
                18 – 4, 17 – 2, 15 – 3]
          C–173 [Less than, circle 18 – 9; Greater than, circle 17 – 2]
          C–174 [Less than, X on 14 – 9; Greater than, X on 17 – 6]
          C–175 [18 – 9]
          C–176 [17 – 6]

PAGES 149–152   EQUAL SETS OF COINS

Mathematical Concepts
- Adding values of coins
- Counting in multiples (5, 10)
- Decomposition of coins
- Assigning a monetary value to a set of coins

VERBAL ANALYSIS STRATEGIES AND ANSWERS

❏   PAGE 149: In these exercises students must match two different sets of coins that have the same value. Before beginning the exercises, discuss the relationships between nickels, dimes, and quarters as on page 126. Discuss with students two strategies that can be used in these exercises: 1) find the value of each set using multiple counting and addition, then match sets with the same value; and 2) match sets by exchanging nickels, dimes, and quarters. Using the first strategy with the Example, the matching sums are 25 + 5 + 4 and 10 + 10 + 10 + 4. Using the second strategy, the quarter and nickel can be replaced by three dimes and thus matched with the set of three dimes and four pennies.

ANSWERS:

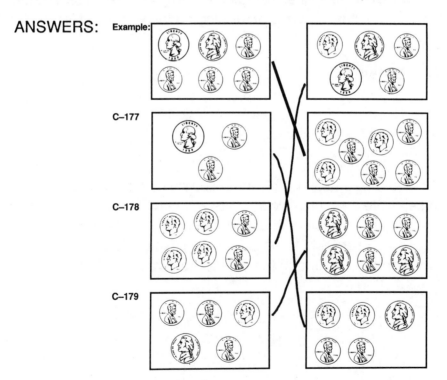

❏   PAGE 150: The activity from page 149 is continued in these exercises. Discuss the two strategies introduced on that page. Note that each given set of coins has two pennies, so sets can be matched by simply considering coin exchanges with nickels, dimes, and quarters. For example, in C–180 there are two possible exchanges: two dimes or four nickels. The second exchange (four nickels) corresponds to the second set in the right column. Using coins or coin-stamps may help students visualize the possible exchanges for each set of coins.

ANSWERS: C–180

C–181

C–182

C–183

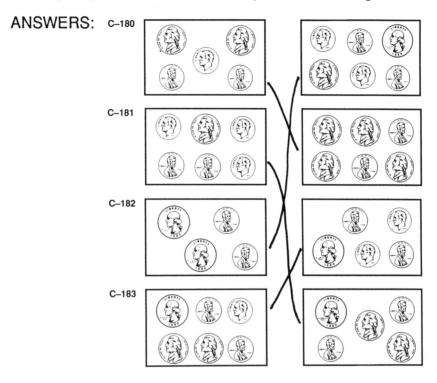

❑   PAGE 151: Students must determine the monetary value of a set of coins and express this value in standard notation. Discuss the need to use strategy 1 from page 149, since the value of the given set is needed. After completing the exercises, ask students what coins must be added or removed from each set to match each number not selected as a solution. In the Example, a dime must be added and a penny removed to make 65, and a penny must be added to make 57. The use of manipulatives is encouraged for the latter activity.

ANSWERS: **C–184** [b. 37]   **C–185** [b. 66]   **C–186** [b. 26]

❑   PAGE 152: These activities are a continuation of those on page 151. Note in these exercises that the coins are randomly placed in the sets. Encourage students to use the strategy of beginning their counting with the coins of largest denomination. For example, in C–188 first count dimes, then nickels, then pennies, as in the sum 10 + 10 + 10 + 5 + 5 + 6 = 46. Some students may need to cross out coins as they are counted to avoid double counting of coins. After completing the exercises, again ask students to alter the sets to match the other two numbers not selected as a solution.

ANSWERS: **C–187** [b. 28]   **C–189** [c. 73]
                      C–188 [b. 46]   **C–190** [b. 62]

PAGES 153–156   GROUPING USING ARRAYS

Mathematical Concepts
- Rectangular arrays
- Counting by multiples
- Multiplication as repeated addition
- Entering data in a table
- Interpreting data from tables
- Combining arrays
- Comparing arrays
- Multiplication facts

VERBAL ANALYSIS STRATEGIES AND ANSWERS

❏   PAGE 153: Multiplication as repeated addition is introduced on this page. Students are asked to count cubes in rectangular arrays by counting cubes in each row and summing these values. Before beginning the exercises, discuss the properties of the arrays. For example, the array in C–192 has five rows and four cubes in each row. When summing the numbers in each table, encourage students to count in multiples of four. After completing the exercises, ask students to use their solutions to verbalize the relationship between rows and columns in counting cubes. For C–192 a student may say, "Five rows of four cubes equals twenty cubes." Note that the arrays on the page represent two 4's, three 4's, four 4's, and five 4's. Ask students how many cubes would be needed to make an array with six 4's.

ANSWERS: **C–191** [4, 4, 4, 4 / 16]   **C–193** [4, 4, 4 / 12]
          C–192 [4, 4, 4, 4, 4 / 20]

❏   PAGE 154: These exercises extend those from page 153 to arrays with rows of six cubes. Discuss the properties of the arrays, and encourage counting in multiples (of six). After completing the exercises, again encourage students to use the data to verbalize the relationship between rows and columns in counting cubes. Also, ask students to compare C–194 and C–197 to C–196. (If C–194 were combined with C–197, the result would be C–196.) Ask students what array would be formed if C–194 were combined with C–195, and how many cubes would be in that array. (It would be a 6 x 6 array with 36 cubes.)

ANSWERS: **C–194** [6, 6 / 12]   **C–196** [6, 6, 6, 6, 6 / 30]
          C–195 [6, 6, 6, 6 / 24]   **C–197** [6, 6, 6 / 18]

❑ PAGE 155: Students are given an array and asked to enter the following data into a table: number of rows, number of cubes in a row, and total number of cubes. Before beginning the exercises, discuss the properties of arrays in terms of rows and the number of cubes in each row. When computing the total number of cubes, multiplication facts may be used. Otherwise, students may use the repeated-addition model from pages 153–154. Some students may need to write the repeated addition as a sum. (In the Example, 3 x 8 = 8 + 8 + 8 = 24.) As on page 154, ask students to compare the Example and C–200.

> ANSWERS: **C–198** [4 x 5 = 20]   **C–200** [5 x 8 = 40]
>   **C–199** [5 x 7 = 35]

❑ PAGE 156: This activity is a continuation of the activity on page 155. Once again, multiplication facts or repeated addition may be used to determine the total number of cubes. After completing the exercises, ask students to compare C–201 and C–202. How many cubes would be used for a 5 x 5 array? Also, compare C–203 and C–204. Discuss the similarities and differences between the two arrays. (They each have six rows, but the array in C–203 has one more cube in each row.)

> ANSWERS: **C–201** [4 x 5 = 20]   **C–203** [6 x 9 = 54]
>   **C–202** [6 x 5 = 30]   **C–204** [6 x 8 = 48]

PAGES 157–160   PRODUCTS/MISSING FACTORS

Mathematical Concepts
- Multiplication facts
- Reverse products (commutativity)
- Arrays as models for multiplication
- Repeated addition
- Missing factors
- Ordering (greater than, less than)

VERBAL ANALYSIS STRATEGIES AND ANSWERS

❑ PAGE 157: Students are asked to match multiplication facts to a given product. (It is assumed for these activities that students are familiar with basic multiplication facts; however, some students may need to revert to the repeated-addition model.) After completing the exercises, ask students to interpret the solution(s) as an array. In the Example, 6 x 8 represents an array containing six rows of eight cubes each. Ask students to describe the array for the reverse product (8 x 6). Also ask students whether there are any other products using single-digit numbers that equal the given number in each exercise. (The only ones are the reverse products.)

ANSWERS: **C–205** [4 x 3, 2 x 6]   **C–209** [5 x 6]
               C–206 [5 x 9]   **C–210** [6 x 3, 2 x 9]
               C–207 [9 x 4, 6 x 6]   **C–211** [6 x 4, 3 x 8]
               C–208 [8 x 2, 4 x 4]

❑ PAGE 158: These exercises use a knowledge of basic multiplication facts to separate a set into two subsets—products less than 40 and products greater than 40. (The activity assumes students have a knowledge of basic multiplication facts.) After completing the exercises, ask students to describe the products in C–212 and C–213 as arrays. Build a 5 x 8 and an 8 x 5 array for reference. Ask students in which set these arrays belong. (Neither, the product is 40.) Ask students to compare the arrays for products in C–212 to the 5 x 8 and 8 x 5 models. Note that the 9 x 3 and 4 x 9 arrays are difficult to compare unless cubes are rearranged. Note also that all other arrays will "fit inside" the model arrays. Do the same for C–213 (here the 6 x 7 and 7 x 7 arrays are difficult to compare).

ANSWERS: **C–212** [2 x 8, 3 x 5, 6 x 3, 4 x 4, 4 x 8, 4 x 9, 9 x 3, 5 x 5]
               C–213 [7 x 8, 7 x 9, 8 x 9, 8 x 8, 7 x 7, 9 x 9, 6 x 7, 6 x 9]
               C–214 [Less than, circle 4 x 9; Greater than, circle 9 x 9]
               C–215 [Less than, X on 3 x 5; Greater than, X on 6 x 7]
               C–216 [4 x 9]
               C–217 [6 x 7]

❑ PAGE 159: The use of multiplication facts continues. (It is assumed that students have a knowledge of basic multiplication facts; however, some students may need to use the strategy of repeated addition to solve the exercises.) Ask students to compare the Example with C–218. How are they similar? Have students verbalize the solutions in terms of arrays, as on page 158. For each exercise ask students to explain the reverse products as arrays. Note that C–221 and C–225 are associated with only one array.

ANSWERS: **C–218** [5]   **C–221** [9]   **C–224** [6]
               C–219 [9]   **C–222** [7]   **C–225** [7]
               C–220 [4]   **C–223** [3]   **C–226** [8]

❑ PAGE 160: This page continues the activity from page 159. Note that each exercise is written in "open sentence" format. Ask students to compare the solutions to C–231 and C–232, and discuss the multiplication property of 1. Note that there are alternate solutions to C–234 and C–236 (4 and 1 in C–234, and 9 and 1 in C–236). Have students compare their solutions in C–234 and C–236 and discuss the alternative ways of writing the products. Also, relate C–233 to C–234. (Note that the answer, 4, in C–233 can be written as 2 x 2, or as 4 x 1 in C–234.) Similarly, compare C–235 and C–236. After discussing these exercises, ask students to write C–227 and C–228 as products of three factors.

ANSWERS: **C–227** [8]   **C–231** [1]   **C–234** [2, 2 4, 1]
          C–228 [10]   **C–232** [1]   **C–235** [9]
          C–229 [5]   **C–233** [4]   **C–236** [3, 3 9, 1]
          C–230 [7]

PAGES 161–164 MULTIPLE OPERATIONS

Mathematical Concepts
- Replacement set
- Open sentences
- Arithmetic operations (+, −, x, ÷)
- Multiple solutions
- Problem solving
- Physical models for verbal problems
- Constructing verbal problems
- Ordering (largest, smallest)

VERBAL ANALYSIS STRATEGIES AND ANSWERS

❑ PAGE 161: These exercises explore the construction of number sentences involving the operations of +, −, x. Remind students that the only numbers they may use in the first two boxes are those in the given replacement set, but the result of the computations may not be in the replacement set. (In the Example, 9 and 8 are in the replacement set, but the sum, 17, is not.) Before beginning the exercises, discuss the Example with students. Ask them to select other pairs of numbers from the replacement set and determine the sums. Why do 9 and 8 make the largest sum? After completing the exercises, ask students to compare their solutions. Discuss why the correct combination is the solution. Note that in C–239 there are seven possible solutions where the difference is 1.

ANSWERS: **C–237** [2 + 3 = 5]   **C–240** [9 x 8 = 72]
          C–238 [9 − 2 = 7]   **C–241** [2 x 3 = 6]
          C–239 [3 − 2 = 1]*

*Note: Six other answers are possible.

❑   PAGE 162: This continues the activity from page 161. Ask students to compare their answers and discuss the solutions as suggested on page 161. Note that C–245, like C–239, has several solutions. Note also that all three numbers in the open sentences in C–243, C–244, and C–247 are from the replacement set. In C–242, what is the largest possible sum if all three numbers used come from the replacement set? (4 + 6 = 10.) Similarly, consider C–245 (multiple solutions with a difference of two) and C–246 (2 x 5 = 10).

ANSWERS: **C–242** [10 + 8 = 18]   **C–245** [3 – 2 = 1]*
          C–243 [2 + 3 = 5]   **C–246** [10 x 8 = 80]
          C–244 [10 – 2 = 8]   **C–247** [2 x 3 = 6]

*Note: Five other answers are possible.

❑   PAGE 163: Students are introduced to the task of identifying the arithmetic operation needed to solve a verbal problem. Before beginning the exercises, discuss the Example. Work with students to construct a physical model to visualize the problem (nine groups of three, or a 9 x 3 matrix of circles). Remind students that 9 x 3 was used earlier to count elements in a 9 x 3 array. Encourage students to make up verbal problems to match the uncircled choices and to visualize physical models as they work on the exercises. After completing the exercises, discuss the solutions in terms of physical models.

ANSWERS: **C–248** [18 – 9]   **C–250** [20 ÷ 4]
          C–249 [12 – 4]   **C–251** [6 + 3]

❑   PAGE 164: This page is a continuation of page 163. As on that page, encourage students to use physical models for solving the exercises. Note that C–255 and C–256 have eight choices rather than four. Note also in C–255 that the given values in the problem are 12 and 3, but a physical model would require dividing a set of twelve into four equal subsets (12 ÷ 4). Similarly, in C–256 a physical model would consist of five groups of ten (5 x 10). After completing the exercises, discuss physical models for some of the choices not selected. In particular, consider models for 12 ÷ 3 in C–255 and for 4 x 10 in C–256.

ANSWERS: **C–252** [4 – 2]   **C–255** [12 ÷ 4]
          C–253 [12 + 6]   **C–256** [5 x 10]
          C–254 [50 x 3]

PAGES 165–168   ROUNDING/ESTIMATING

Mathematical Concepts
- Counting in multiples (10)
- The number line
- Locating points on the number line
- Rounding to the nearest 10 (and nearest 100)
- Addition facts
- Classification (by multiples)

VERBAL ANALYSIS STRATEGIES AND ANSWERS

❑   PAGE 165: A series of exercises are introduced here involving rounding numbers to the nearest 10 and the nearest 100. Discuss the construction of a number line starting at 0 and increasing in multiples of 10 to 80. This number line may be used as a model for the exercises on the page. As a strategy to solve these exercises, have students locate the given number in the exercises on the model number line. In the Example, 8 is located between 0 and 10 on the number line. It will be visually clear to most students that 8 is closer to 10 than to any other multiple of 10. In some exercises the solution may not be visually clear. For example, in C–261 the value 76 is between 70 and 80 on the number-line model. If students can't tell if 76 is closer to 70 or to 80, ask questions like: How far is 76 from 70? How far from 80? Therefore, the solution is 80. If necessary, mark the units between 70 and 80 on the model number line to find the exact location of 76. An alternate strategy is to locate the midpoint between multiples of 10 (in C–261 this is 75) and compare the given number to the midpoint.

ANSWERS: **C–257** [10]   **C–260** [50]   **C–263** [30]
                C–258 [20]   **C–261** [80]
                C–259 [20]   **C–262** [10]

❑   PAGE 166: This page extends the activity from page 165. In the first set of exercises students are not given multiples of 10 to choose from, but must identify the closest multiple of 10 to the given number. Refer to the number-line model and the strategies used on page 165. The second set of exercises on the page requires the construction of a number-line model using multiples of 100 (from 0 to 700). Encourage students to locate the given numbers between two multiples of 100 on the number line and to identify the closest multiple. Locating midpoints between the hundreds on the number line may assist in determining the solutions.

ANSWERS: **C–264** [10]   **C–268** [90]   **C–271** [700]
              C–265 [60]   **C–269** [100]   **C–272** [400]
              C–266 [50]   **C–270** [400]   **C–273** [600]
              C–267 [20]

❑ PAGE 167: These exercises extend the activity from page 166. Two possible strategies can be used: 1) the number-line model or 2) arithmetic comparisons to 40 and 50. In the number-line model, a number line from 30 to 60 can be used with the strategies outlined on page 165. In the second strategy, ask questions like: How far is 41 from 40? How far from 50? Is 41 closer to 40 or to 50?

ANSWERS: **C–274** [41, 40, 39, 43, 37, 42, 38, 44]
              C–275 [52, 46, 53, 50, 47, 51, 48, 49]

❑ PAGE 168: As an extension of the activity on page 167, students are required to complete sums before rounding and sorting them into subsets. (This task assumes students have a knowledge of basic addition facts.) After completing the sums, students may use either of the two strategies discussed on page 167 to determine whether sums are closer to 10 or to 20.

ANSWERS: **C–276** [3 + 6, 4 + 9, 9 + 5, 6 + 8, 8 + 2 , 5 + 7, 7 + 4,
                    6 + 6, 9 + 2, 7 + 7, 6 + 7, 5 + 8]
        C–277 [10 + 7, 11 + 10, 8 + 9, 7 + 9, 6 + 10, 9 + 10,
                    8 + 8, 9 + 9]

PAGES 169–170   MULTIPLES OF 10 AND 100

Mathematical Concepts
- Multiplication facts
- Products using multiples of 10 (and 100)
- Estimating products
- Rounding to nearest 10

VERBAL ANALYSIS STRATEGIES AND ANSWERS

❑ PAGE 169: This activity explores the effect on products of multiplying one factor by 10 (or by 100). The exercises assume students know their basic multiplication facts and are able to multiply a single-digit number by 10 or 100. These ideas are extended on this page to multiplying two-digit numbers by 10 (or 100). In the Example, discuss with students that 5 x 30 may be written as 5 x 3 x 10, which is 15 x 10. Likewise, in C–281, 4 x 200 may be written as 4 x 2 x 100 = 8 x 100. After completing the exercises, ask students to compare the number of zeros in the two products in each exercise, C–278 through C–282. What is the pattern? (There is one additional zero when multiplying by a multiple of 10, and there are two additional zeros with multiples of 100.)

ANSWERS: **C–278** [16, 160]   **C–281** [8, 800]   **C–284** [720]
          C–279 [36, 360]   **C–282** [28, 2800] **C–285** [3500]
          C–280 [30, 300]   **C–283** [900]   **C–286** [4800]

❏ PAGE 170: These exercises combine the tasks of rounding to 10's (from pages 165–168) and the use of multiples of 10 (from page 169). Students are asked to estimate products by a two-step process: 1) rounding a two-digit number to the nearest 10, and 2) multiplying the rounded answer by a given number. After completing the exercises, ask students to compare the actual products of the exercises to the products in the boxes. In the Example, compare 95 to 100. What is the difference between the actual and estimated products? (The estimate is five more than the actual product.) Ask students which is easier, estimating products or computing products. Note that estimating is a mental computation.

ANSWERS: **C–287** [50, 300]   **C–289** [40, 280]   **C–291** [60, 240]
          C–288 [70, 560]   **C–290** [20, 180]

INTRODUCTION TO MEASUREMENT

The **Measurement** section of **MATHEMATICAL REASONING** encourages students to integrate numeric and geometric concepts through a series of activities focusing on measurement problems involving length and area. Exploratory activities that introduce a unit of length (a unit segment on geoboards, grids, or tiles) and a unit of area (unit squares on geoboards or grids) are designed to assist students in developing an understanding of the fundamental concepts of measurement.

Activities that introduce the concept of measurement as it relates to length ask students to use both counting techniques and computation as strategies. The process of measurement is applied to a variety of problem-solving situations and is used as a basis for comparison and estimation. Activities dealing with length include:

- comparing or determining lengths of segments and paths using counting and computation
- drawing paths on geoboards and grids
- using estimation to compare paths

These ideas are extended to closed figures by activities considering the distance around figures (perimeter), finding missing lengths (indirect measure), and other problem-solving situations.

Counting and computation are also used as strategies to find solutions to activities that introduce the measurement of area. The activities dealing with area include:

INTRODUCTION TO MEASUREMENT
(continued)

- comparing and determining areas of figures using decomposition (units and half units) and composition of two or more figures
- drawing figures of a given area on geoboards or grids
- using estimation

Reference is again made in the individual activities to specific manipulative materials that are appropriate for assisting in the conceptual development of measurement ideas. In addition, reproducible pages of geoboard designs and grids appear at the end of this manual for use in practice or extending activities.

PAGES 171–174 FINDING LENGTHS BY COUNTING

Mathematical Concepts
- Decomposition
- Missing-addend model
- Finding missing addends
- Using linear measure
- Unit length
- Number sentences
- Lengths of paths

VERBAL ANALYSIS STRATEGIES AND ANSWERS

❑ PAGE 171: This activity introduces the task of comparing lengths using the concept of linear measurement. The exercises follow similar activities from the **Operations** section dealing with the missing-addend model. Several strategies discussed on those previous pages (139–141) may be employed, including: 1) decomposition of sets, 2) pairing squares (one-to-one correspondence), and 3) finding missing addends by counting unit squares. After completing the exercises, ask students to discuss them in terms of either decomposition of sets or the missing-addend model. In the Example, a rod of 8 may be decomposed to rods of 5, 3. Also, the solution (3) is the missing addend.

ANSWERS: **D–1** [b. 3]   **D–4** [a. 2]   **D–6** [a. 3]
D–2 [c. 2]   **D–5** [b. 2]   **D–7** [c. 1]
D–3 [a. 4]

❑ PAGE 172: Students are encouraged to use the missing-addend model and linear measure to make lengths of 10. In the missing-addend model, students must compare the given rod to a rod of length 10. If a physical model (a rod of length 10) is needed, refer to the rod in exercise D–14 on this page. After completing the exercises, ask students to express the solutions as number sentences. In the Example, 4 + 6 = 10.

ANSWERS: **D–8** [a. 7]   **D–11** [c. 1]   **D–13** [b. 2]
D–9 [c. 4]   **D–12** [a. 5]   **D–14** [c. 0]
D–10 [b. 8]

❑ PAGE 173: These exercises extend the activities on pages 171–172 to paths that are not linear. As before, lengths of paths can be determined by counting unit squares. After completing the exercises, ask students to compare the path in

D–15 to the path in the Example. How could the path in D–15 be made the same as the Example? (By adding one square to the A end of the path and two squares to the B end.) This illustrates the missing-addend model (11 + 3 = 14). Similarly, compare D–16 to D–17 and D–18 to D–19. Comparisons can also be made between these pairs of figures in terms of congruence and geometric motions.

ANSWERS: **D–15** [11]   **D–17** [9]   **D–19** [15]
                D–16 [8]   **D–18** [17]

❑   PAGE 174: More complex figures are added to extend the exercises on page 173. Before beginning the page of exercises, ask students to compare the path in the Example (fifteen squares) to the path in D–20. How can the two paths be made to match (congruent)? (By adding two squares to the horizontal part of the Example.) What then is the length of this path? (15 + 2 = 17, which is the length pictured in D–20.) Similarly, ask students to relate D–21 to D–22 and D–23 to D–24 as they complete the exercises.

ANSWERS: **D–20** [17]   **D–22** [16]   **D–24** [18]
                D–21 [12]   **D–23** [14]

PAGES 175–178   FINDING LENGTHS USING SUMS

Mathematical Concepts
- Length of a path
- Sums of 10
- Sums of 8
- Comparing lengths
- Congruence of figures

VERBAL ANALYSIS STRATEGIES AND ANSWERS

❑   PAGE 175: The arithmetic operation of addition is used in this activity to find the length of a path. After completing the exercises, ask the students to verbalize the relationship between the paths with X's. (All of the sums are 10.) Ask students to write these relations as number sentences using addition. Are there any other two lengths that would make a path of 10? (Yes, 1 + 9.) How can the path in D–27 be changed so the length is 10? Compare the result to the figures in the Example and in D–26. Similarly consider the path in D–29.

ANSWERS: **D–25** [10, X]   **D–27** [9]   **D–29** [11]
                D–26 [10, X]   **D–28** [10, X]

❑ PAGE 176: This activity is a continuation of the exercises on page 175. Ask students to verbalize again the relationship between the paths with X's. (All sums are 8.) Also, ask students to write these relations as number sentences using addition. Are there any other two lengths that would make a path of 8? (No.) How can the path in D–30 be changed so the length is 8? Compare the result to both the Example and D–32. Similarly consider the path in D–34.

ANSWERS: **D–30** [9]   **D–32** [8, X]   **D–34** [7]
          D–31 [8, X]   **D–33** [8, X]

❑ PAGE 177: Counting is used to determine the lengths of paths in these exercises. The geoboard design defines the unit for counting and allows the construction of more complex paths. After completing the exercises, discuss with students the Example and D–37. Are they the same length? (Yes.) Are they congruent? (Yes, the Example can be flipped or turned to match D–37.) Similarly, discuss the pairs D–36 and D–39, and D–38 and D–35. Note that these pairs have equal lengths but are not congruent.

ANSWERS:

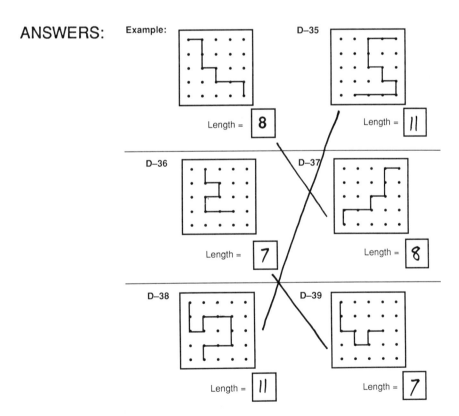

❑ PAGE 178: This page continues the activity from page 177 of counting on the geoboard to determine lengths of paths. Once again, compare paths of equal length. Are any of these pairs congruent? (No.)

ANSWERS:

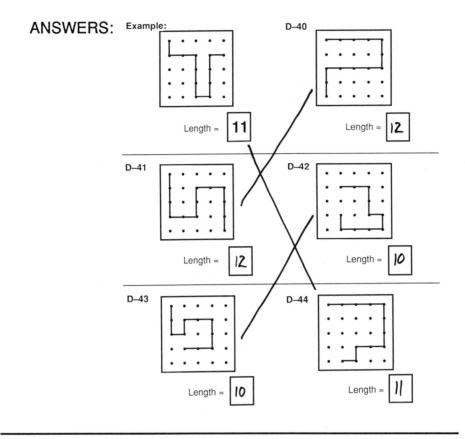

Example:

Length = 11

D–40

Length = 12

D–41

Length = 12

D–42

Length = 10

D–43

Length = 10

D–44

Length = 11

PAGES 179–184   DRAWING PATHS:
EQUAL / LONGER / SHORTER

Mathematical Concepts
- Using linear measure
- Finding lengths of paths
- Comparing paths of equal length
- Constructing paths of given length
- Congruence
- Constructing paths (shorter / longer)
- Verifying solutions

VERBAL ANALYSIS STRATEGIES AND ANSWERS

❑   PAGE 179: In these exercises students are given the two endpoints of a path and must construct a path with a given length. The geoboard design is used for reference and to provide the unit of length. Stress that only horizontal or vertical lines may be used in the paths. In all exercises (except D–46) the shortest path from A to B is not a solution. For most students, construction of a suitable path will be done by trial and error. Here the use of a geoboard or additional dot paper may be necessary for experimentation. After completing the exercises, have students compare their solutions. Do any paths match (congruent)? Ask students to verify that the paths are the correct length. Note that multiple solutions are possible for the exercises in this section (pages 179–184).

ANSWERS:

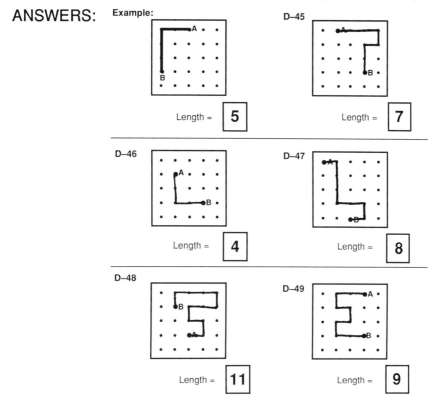

☐ PAGE 180: As an extension of the activity from page 179, students must first determine the length of a given path, then construct another path of equal length. Stress again that only vertical and horizontal lines are to be used. As before, the use of a geoboard or additional dot paper may be necessary for experimentation. Discuss the Example with the students. Are there any other paths from X to B that have a length of 5? (Yes, there are several.) Have students compare their solutions. Are any paths congruent? Ask students to verify that the paths are the correct length.

ANSWERS:

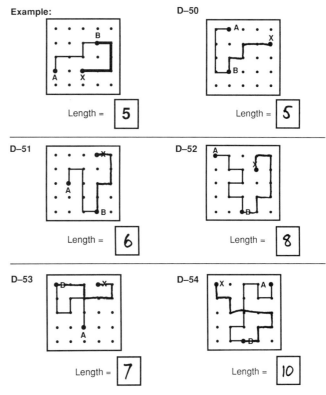

❏   PAGE 181: This page extends the activity from page 180 to constructing paths that are *one unit longer* than a given path. Follow the suggestions from the two previous pages. Make sure students verify that their paths are one unit longer than the given path.

ANSWERS:

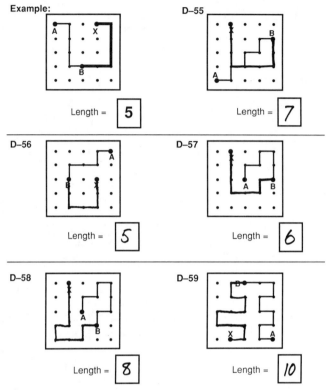

❏   PAGE 182: The activity from page 181 is extended here to constructing paths that are *two units shorter* than a given path. Follow the suggestions from pages 179–180 and have students verify their solutions. Discuss with students that any solution to the Example must have a length of 3. Is a path of length 3 the shortest path that can be drawn from X to B? (Yes.) Ask students to determine which exercises have solutions whose paths are the shortest distance from X to B. (D–60 and D–61.)

ANSWERS:

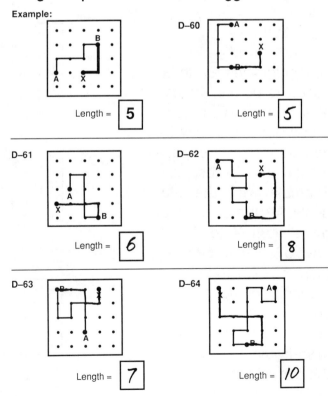

                                       P.O. BOX 448, PACIFIC GROVE, CA 93950

❑ PAGE 183: These exercises extend the activity from page 182 by requiring that the path drawn pass through a third point. This increases the complexity of the task of finding a suit-able path to match the given length. Because of the complex-ity of the task, students must use trial and error and, as in earlier activi-ties, geoboards or dot paper may be helpful. Have students verify that their solutions have the correct length and pass through point X.

ANSWERS:

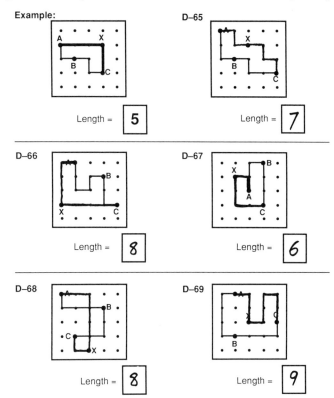

❑ PAGE 184: The tasks from pages 182 and 183 are combined in this activity. The paths in a student's solution must pass through a third point *and* be two units shorter than the length of the given path. Geoboards or dot paper may be needed for ex-perimentation. Have stu-dents compare solutions and verify their answers.

ANSWERS:

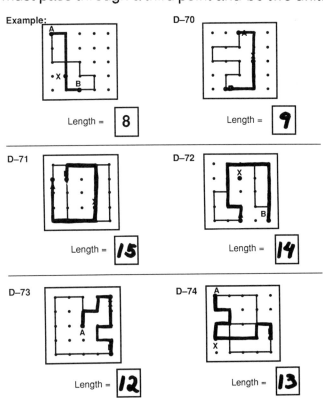

PAGES 185–188   COMPARING PATHS: EQUAL / LONGER / SHORTER

Mathematical Concepts
- Comparing lengths of paths
- Finding the length of a path
- Strategies for comparing lengths
- Comparing the hypoteneuse to the legs of a right triangle

VERBAL ANALYSIS STRATEGIES AND ANSWERS

❏ PAGE 185: Students are asked to compare lengths of paths that are constructed with horizontal and vertical segments. In these exercises there are no reference points to define a unit of measure as in the geoboard activities. Three strategies can be discussed for solving these exercises. 1) Find the smallest segment in the two paths being compared and use this as a unit. Then subdivide longer segments into units and count. In the Example, using the first segment in Bill's path as a unit, Bill's path is ten units and Chuck's path is eight units. 2) Cross out pieces in the two paths that match or have the same length until one path is exhausted. In the Example, after matching pieces of the paths, Chuck's path is exhausted and Bill's path has two units left. 3) Extend the horizontal and vertical segments in the figures to form a grid and use the resulting units in this grid to count the lengths of the paths.

ANSWERS: **D–75** [Jose]   **D–77** [Carla]   **D–79** [Nancy]
        D–76 [Anita]   **D–78** [Hector]

❏ PAGE 186: This page extends the exercises from page 185 by asking students to identify the shorter of two paths. Discuss the three strategies introduced on page 185. In the Example, using the first segment of Neil's path as a unit, Neil's path is seven units and Carlos' path is eight. Also, the four horizontal pieces of Neil's path match the horizontal pieces of Carlos' path, and Carlos' path has four vertical units compared to Neil's three units. Note that drawing a grid for this figure makes the counting process easier.

ANSWERS: **D–80** [Sara]   **D–82** [Andrea]   **D–84** [Juan]
        D–81 [Andy]   **D–83** [Keith]

❏ PAGE 187: The activities from pages 185–186 are extended here by introducing diagonal segments in the paths to be compared. Each diagonal is the hypoteneuse of a right triangle (with sides of one unit). Discuss the fact that in a right triangle the sum of the lengths of the two legs is longer than the hypoteneuse (or diagonal path). Also, the hypoteneuse is longer than either leg. Because the diagonal segments are not units, counting is not a possible strategy. Discuss the strategy of matching pieces of paths in the Example. In the triangle, Bob's two segments are longer than the diagonal in Lorenzo's path. Also, Bob's path has two other unit segments compared to one in Lorenzo's. Note that in D–89 a vertical line must be constructed to create a right triangle for comparison. Discuss with students that the solution to D–86 must be one of the circled answers (similarly for D–90). The answer to D–87 will be the shorter of the uncircled choices (similarly for D–91).

ANSWERS: **D–85** [Michelle]   **D–88** [Chris]   **D–90** [Ann]
             D–86 [Bob]   **D–89** [Ann]   **D–91** [Oscar]
             D–87 [Lorenzo]

❑ PAGE 188: These exercises extend those from page 187 by including more than one diagonal segment in some paths being compared. As on page 187, discuss the drawing of segments to complete right triangles in the figures and the relationships between the hypoteneuse and legs of a right triangle. Discuss the Example. Note that Beth's path has a length of five units, and Michael's path has three unit segments plus two diagonal segments. Since the diagonals are longer than one unit, Michael's path is longer.

ANSWERS: **D–92** [John]   **D–95** [Kum]   **D–97** [Ken]
             D–93 [Michael]   **D–96** [Chris]   **D–98** [Kum]
             D–94 [John]

PAGES 189–200 DISTANCE AROUND FIGURES

Mathematical Concepts
- Perimeter by counting
- Perimeters by adding lengths
- Matching figures by perimeter
- Combining shapes
- Indirect measurement (finding missing lengths)
- Constructing figures with a given perimeter

VERBAL ANALYSIS STRATEGIES AND ANSWERS

❑ PAGE 189: This page introduces a series of activities dealing with perimeter (distance around a closed figure). Because the figures are closed, there is no obvious starting point to compute lengths as in previous paths. These exercises may be viewed as counting tasks. Discuss the importance of marking (with a check or an X) the starting point when counting units. The geoboard design defines a unit segment and aids in counting. Encourage students to start at several different points and go in different directions when counting. After completing the exercises, have students compare the Example and D–101, D–99 and D–100, and D–102 and D–103. (These pairs have different shapes but identical perimeters.) Also, ask students to determine the length of each side in a figure and sum these lengths. Compare this sum to the result from counting (they should be the same). In the Example, 3 + 2 + 1 + 1 + 3 + 2 + 1 + 1 = 14.

ANSWERS: **D–99** [12]   **D–101** [14]   **D–103** [16]
           D–100 [12]   **D–102** [16]

❑ PAGE 190: Figures drawn on a 5 x 5 grid instead of a geoboard are used to continue the activity from page 189. Stress the need to mark a starting point for the counting process for closed figures. After completing the exercises, compare the Example and D–107 (also compare D–104 and D–108). Ask students to compute the distance by adding the lengths of the sides of each figure. In the Example, 2 + 2 + 1 + 1 + 2 + 2 + 1 + 1 = 12.

ANSWERS: **D–104** [14]   **D–106** [8]   **D–108** [14]
           D–105 [16]   **D–107** [12]

❑ PAGE 191: The activity of determining perimeter is extended to figures that are not placed on grids or geoboards. Since the lengths of sides are given, the perimeter must be computed by summing the lengths of the sides. Again, stress the need to indicate a starting point when computing sums.

ANSWERS: **D–109** [16]   **D–111** [12]
           D–110 [18]   **D–112** [20]

❑ PAGE 192: As a continuation of the activity from page 191, students must first compute the perimeter of each figure by summing, then match figures with the same perimeters. Compare the matched figures in the Example. Can the segments in the figure in the left column be rearranged to create the matching figure in the right column? (Yes, slide the vertical segment of length 1 to the right and the horizontal segment of length 2 upward.) Similarly, discuss a possible rearrangement in D–113.

ANSWERS:

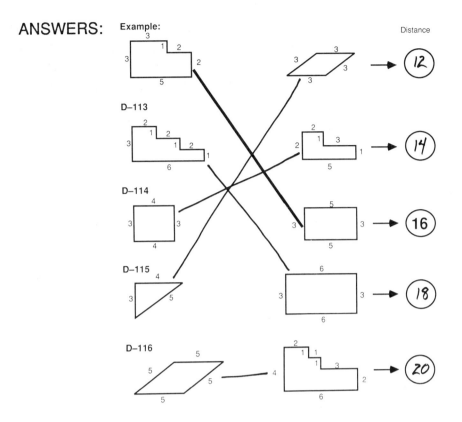

☐ PAGE 193: This page extends the activity of determining perimeter to figures formed by combining two shapes. The geoboard design is used to define a unit segment and to assist in counting. Discuss the concept of perimeter and the need to ignore the dotted lines in each figure. Once again, stress the need to identify a starting point for counting. The strategy of summing length of sides can also be used and is easiest in D–118 and D–121. After completing the exercises, ask the students to compare the Example and D–121. (Both are constructed from the same two shapes.) Which has the smaller perimeter? (The rectangle.) Similarly compare D–117 and D–118.

ANSWERS: **D–117** [12]   **D–119** [12]   **D–121** [14]
                     D–118 [10]   **D–120** [16]

☐ PAGE 194: The activity from page 193 is extended in these exercises by joining three rectangles to form a variety of figures. Stress the need to ignore the dotted lines when computing the perimeter and the need to identify a starting point. Once the exercises are completed, ask students which shape has the smallest perimeter. (The rectangle.) Are there other figures that can be formed using the three rectangles? (Yes.) What are their perimeters? (Note that 10, 12, and 14 are the only possible perimeters.)

ANSWERS: **D–122** [14]   **D–124** [12]   **D–126** [14]
                     D–123 [14]   **D–125** [10]

❑   PAGE 195: This page extends the activity of computing perimeter to figures made by combining shapes other than squares and rectangles. Also, the strategy of counting on a grid is no longer possible. To compute perimeters, students can count by multiples of two or use addition of lengths. Remind students to ignore the dotted lines when computing the perimeter. The basic shape used in these figures is the (blue) pattern block. If pattern blocks are available, ask students if other figures can be constructed. What are their perimeters? (The only possible perimeters are 12 and 16.)

ANSWERS: **D–127** [16]   **D–128** [12]   **D–129** [16]

❑   PAGE 196: Forming figures with three different shapes extends the activity from page 195. The shapes used are pattern block shapes (red, blue, and green). If the blocks are available, ask students to construct different figures and compute the perimeters of these figures. Further discuss both the concept of perimeter and the fact that the joined segments of the figures should not be counted in the perimeter. Note that the only two perimeters possible using these three shapes are 12 and 16.

ANSWERS: **D–130** [16]   **D–131** [16]   **D–132** [16]

❑   PAGE 197: These exercises reverse the previous activities by giving the perimeter and asking students to complete a closed figure with this perimeter. Note that there are multiple solutions to the Example. Ask students to find other solutions to the Example. Since completing these exercises requires trial and error, providing grid paper for experimentation would be helpful to the students. After completing the exercises, ask students to compare their solutions. Is more than one solution possible? (Yes, except for D–134.)

ANSWERS:

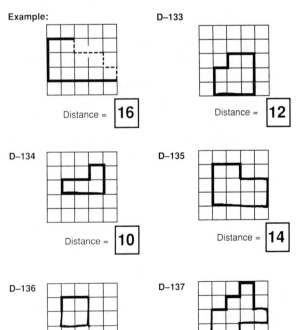

Example: Distance = 16

D–133   Distance = 12

D–134   Distance = 10

D–135   Distance = 14

D–136   Distance = 8

D–137   Distance = 18

❑ PAGE 198: This is an extension of the previous page, with students asked again to construct an entire closed figure for a given perimeter. In this activity, however, grid paper is replaced by the geoboard design.

There are multiple solutions to each exercise; therefore, trial and error is important. Providing dot paper or geoboards for experimentation could be helpful to students. After completing the exercises, ask students to compare their solutions. Is it possible to construct a rectangle as a solution to each exercise? (No, a rectangle of perimeter 18 will not fit on the geoboard in D–141.)

ANSWERS:

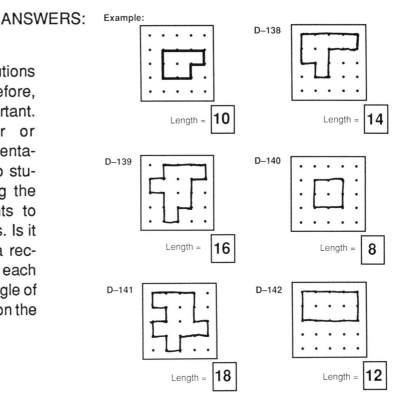

❑ PAGE 199: In these exercises the closed figures pictured are not on grid paper or geoboards. Students are asked to find the missing lengths of sides of figures when some lengths are given (indirect measurement). Before beginning the exercises, discuss a strategy for finding the missing lengths. In the Example, ask students to compare the vertical lengths on the left side of the figure (2 + 1) to those on the right (2 + 1). Will they always be the same? (Yes.) Similarly, ask students to compare the horizontal distances: 4 + 2 on the top and 1 + ? on the bottom. Will these two values always be the same? (Yes.) What is the missing length? (4 + 2 = 1 + ? gives the missing length 5.) Ask students to employ this strategy to find the missing vertical and horizontal lengths in the exercises.

ANSWERS:

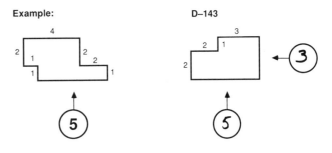

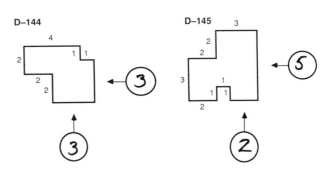

❑ PAGE 200: This page extends the activity of determining perimeter to figures that are not drawn on grids or geoboards. The perimeters must be determined by summing the lengths of the sides. Again, in each exercise some lengths must be determined before summing is possible. Before beginning the exercises, discuss the strategy from page 199 for finding the missing lengths. In the Example, the vertical distance on the left is 2 + 2 = 4, and the given vertical distance on the right is 2 + 1 = 3. Therefore, the missing vertical length is 1. Comparing the horizontal distances (3 + 2 = 5 on the bottom and 2 + 1 = ? on top), the missing horizontal length is 2. Note that each exercise can be drawn on grid paper (5 x 5). Ask students to find other figures with perimeters of 18 that can be drawn on grid paper.

ANSWERS:

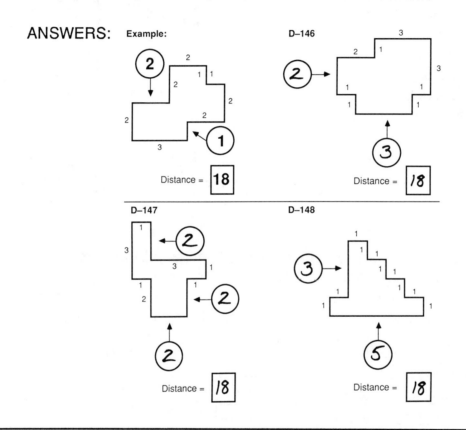

PAGES 201–210 AREA BY COUNTING

Mathematical Concepts
- Area by counting
- Counting strategies
- Area of a rectangle
- Figures of equal area
- Subdivision into unit squares
- Completing rectangles
- Indirect measurement

VERBAL ANALYSIS STRATEGIES AND ANSWERS

❑ PAGE 201: These exercises introduce counting strategies for finding the areas of figures which are subdivided into unit squares. Discuss different counting techniques: 1) consecutive counting (students may need to check off squares as they are counted); 2) counting the number of squares in the rows and summing (in the Example, 3 + 5 + 2 = 10); and 3) counting the number of squares in the columns and summing (in D–153, 3 + 3 + 3 + 3 = 12). After completing the exercises, discuss rearranging the unit squares in the figures to create rectangles. In the Example, the bottom two squares can be moved to the top row, making a 2 x 5 rectangle. Ask students how they would rearrange squares to create rectangles in exercises D–149, D–152, and D–153. Also ask students to compare the figures in D–150 and D–151. If two squares were added to the left side and right side of D–150, the result would be D–151. (Note that 2 + 9 + 2 = 13.)

ANSWERS: **D–149** [12]   **D–151** [13]   **D–153** [12]
                 D–150 [9]   **D–152** [12]

❑ PAGE 202: The activity from page 201 is continued here. Stress the strategies of counting squares in rows or columns and summing. After completing the exercises, discuss the rearrangement of unit squares to form rectangles. In the Example, two squares must be moved to form a rectangle. The top square can be moved to the left side of the second row, and the lower right square can be moved to the right side of that row. This makes a 3 x 5 rectangle. Ask students how they would rearrange squares to create rectangles in exercises D–154, D–155, D–157, and D–158. Some students may have difficulty visualizing these rearrangements. Manipulatives (cubes or tiles) may be useful for physically rearranging the unit squares.

ANSWERS: **D–154** [16]   **D–156** [13]   **D–158** [16]
                 D–155 [15]   **D–157** [14]

❑ PAGE 203: These exercises focus on the strategy of counting squares in rows and columns to find the area of rectangles. This activity relates to the previous activities of counting arrays (pages 153–156). After completing the exercises, encourage students to verbalize the data as multiplication relationships. In the Example, three rows of four equals twelve (3 x 4 = 12). Ask students to compare the Example and D–159 (3 x 4 = 4 x 3). Also compare D–160 and D–161.

ANSWERS:

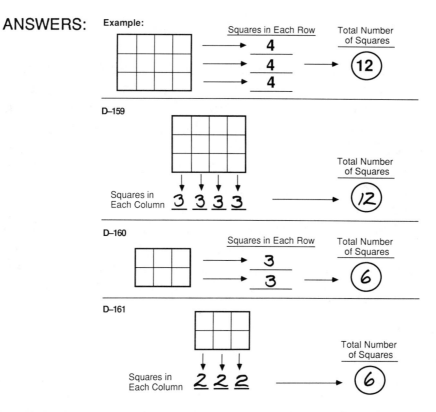

PAGE 204: In this continuation of page 203, encourage students once again to use the data to verbalize the counting strategy. In the Example, two rows of five equals ten (2 x 5 = 10). Compare the Example and D–162; also compare D–163 and D–164.

ANSWERS:

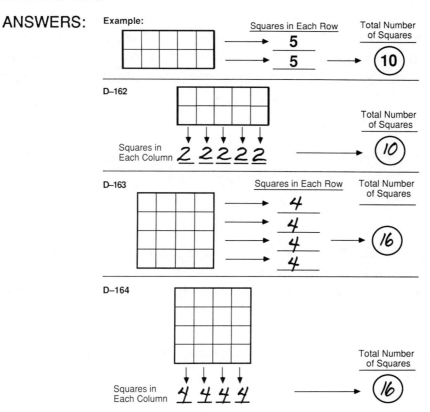

❑   PAGE 205: This page continues the activity of finding the area of figures and introduces the task of subdividing figures into unit squares. The geoboard design defines the unit square and aids in the subdivision process. After students subdivide the figures into unit squares, suggest they use the counting strategies from pages 201–202. After completing the exercises, discuss rearranging squares to create rectangles. (This can be done in D–166, D–167, and D–169.) Note in D–168 that if a 2 x 5 rectangle is formed, it will not fit on the geoboard.

ANSWERS: **D–165** [8]   **D–167** [9]   **D–169** [12]
           D–166 [6]   **D–168** [10]

❑   PAGE 206: Page 205 is continued in this activity. After completing the exercises, discuss rearranging squares to create rectangles. (This can be done in D–173, D–174, and D–175.) Students could create these rectangles on dot paper or the geoboard and compare their results. Note in D–170 and D–171 that if a 2 x 5 rectangle is formed, it will not fit on the geoboard.

ANSWERS: **D–170** [10]   **D–172** [7]   **D–174** [8]
           D–171 [10]   **D–173** [6]   **D–175** [8]

❑   PAGE 207: The earlier task of rearranging squares is extended to adding squares to create a rectangle. Completing the rectangle involves extending two sides of the given figure. To count the number of squares added to the figure, some students may need to subdivide into unit squares. After completing the exercises, ask students to find the area of the rectangle in the Example. (12) How could the area of the original figure be found using the area of the rectangle and the solution? (12 – 4 = 8) Have students verify that the area of the original figure is 8. Compare the rectangles in the Example and D–177, and in D–179 and D–180. (They are congruent and have areas of 12.) Ask students to compute the areas of the original figures using the area 12 and their solutions. Also, ask students to verify their answers by counting squares in the original figures.

ANSWERS:

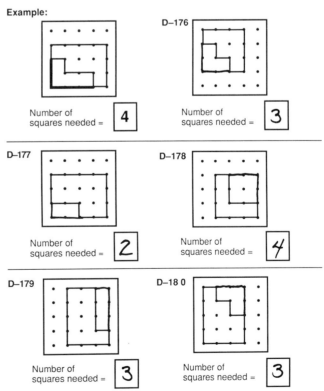

Example:
Number of squares needed = 4

D–176
Number of squares needed = 3

D–177
Number of squares needed = 2

D–178
Number of squares needed = 4

D–179
Number of squares needed = 3

D–180
Number of squares needed = 3

❑   PAGE 208: This is a continuation of the previous page, without the use of the geoboard design for reference. Discuss three steps that could be used to complete the exercises: 1) determine the lengths of the dotted lines using the missing length strategy from pages 199–200; 2) use these values to subdivide the added region into unit squares; and 3) count the unit squares in the added region or regions. After completing the exercises, discuss the Example with students. What are the dimensions of the rectangle? (3 x 5) What is its area? (15) Using the area (15) and the solution (5), find the area of the original figure. (15 – 5 = 10) Repeat this activity with each exercise.

ANSWERS: **D–181** [3]   **D–183** [3]   **D–185** [7]
                  D–182 [3]   **D–184** [3]

❑   PAGE 209: In these exercises students must determine the areas of figures using the techniques of subdividing and counting. Unit segments are marked on each side of the figures, allowing students to construct a grid that subdivides the figures into unit squares. This strategy is similar to an earlier one suggested in the activities on pages 185–186. After completing the exercises, encourage students to verbalize the areas of the Example and D–186 in terms of products (3 x 4 and 2 x 6). What rearrangements could be used to match D–189 to the Example? What rearrangements could be used to make D–190 match the Example or D–186?

ANSWERS:

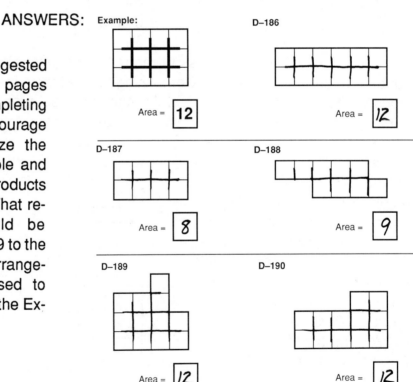

❑   PAGE 210: This activity is a continuation of page 209. Note that D–192 is a 3 x 5 rectangle. How could the unit squares in D–193 and D–195 be rearranged to match the rectangle in D–192? Manipulatives (cubes or tiles) may assist in describing these rearrangements.

ANSWERS:

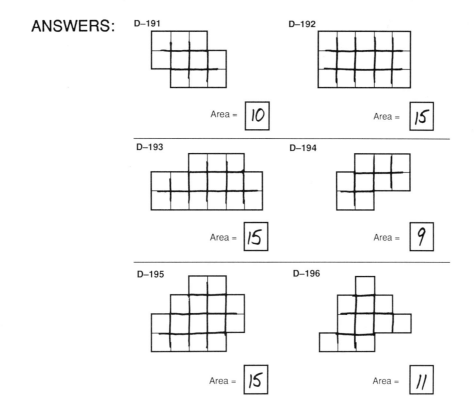

D–191   Area = 10

D–192   Area = 15

D–193   Area = 15

D–194   Area = 9

D–195   Area = 15

D–196   Area = 11

PAGES 211–218   COMPUTING AREA

Mathematical Concepts
- Matching congruent figures
- Area by counting
- Subdividing figures into unit squares
- Area of a region by summing parts

VERBAL ANALYSIS STRATEGIES AND ANSWERS

❑ PAGE 211: Students must locate a figure which is embedded in a more complex figure and determine its area. They may use two different strategies in completing these exercises. Some students may be able to visualize the subdivision of each figure into unit squares. This approach is similar to the activity on page 208. Other students may need to use the geoboard design to subdivide figures into units. In this approach, students must match the given figure with a congruent figure on the geoboard. It is possible to lose sight of the original figure when subdividing the geoboard figure. Suggest that students first outline the matching figures or use dotted lines when subdividing. After completing the exercises, ask if the area of each region pictured on the geoboard has been found (match figures to the geoboard design). Compare the sum of the four areas found on the page to the area of the geoboard. (The area of the geoboard is 4 x 4, and the sum of the areas is 4 + 3 + 4 + 5.)

ANSWERS: **D–197** [3]   **D–198** [4]   **D–199** [5]

❑ PAGE 212: This is an extension of the exercises on page 211, using an enlarged geoboard (5 x 7 dots). Note the two possible approaches discussed on page 211. After completing the exercises, ask students to compare the area of the geoboard (4 x 6 = 24) to the sum of the areas of the four pictured figures. Why are they not equal? Ask students to find the shapes in the geoboard design that have not been included in the sum. What are their areas? (1 and 4)

ANSWERS: **D–200** [5]   **D–202** [4]
          D–201 [5]   **D–203** [5]

❑ PAGE 213: These activities extend those from pages 211–212 to regions that cannot be constructed on a geoboard design. Now it is impossible for students to determine the area of the given figures without matching them to congruent figures in the given square. Discuss previous strategies for matching congruent figures (i.e., number of sides, right angles, lengths of sides, and parallelism). Make sure students have matched figures that are congruent. Discuss with them the task of computing the area of the given square (the sum of the areas of the five regions). Identify the region that is not pictured in the Example or the exercises.

ANSWERS: **D–204** [4]   **D–205** [4]   **D–206** [2]

❑ PAGE 214: As an extension of the activity on page 213, students must now find a figure in the given square that is composed of two or more regions (union of regions). Note that each figure has a unique area, but some figures may be matched with two different congruent regions in the square. In the Example, the given figure is congruent to the right triangle formed by the left and bottom sides of the square and the diagonal (area = 4 + 1 + 3 = 8). The given figure is also congruent to the right triangle formed by the top and right sides of the square and the diagonal (area = 3 + 5 = 8). In exercises D–207 and D–208, ask students to find two different congruent figures in the square that match. In D–209 there is only one matching congruent figure in the given square. After completing the exercises, ask students to compare the area of the Example to the area of the square. (The Example is one-half the area of the square.) Similarly compare D–207 to the square. (D–207 is also one-half the area of the square.)

ANSWERS: **D–207** [8]   **D–208** [5]   **D–209** [9]

❑ PAGE 215: The geoboard design is used to introduce the computation of area using half-units. Discuss the subdivision of the unit square into two equal parts (two one-half units of area equal one square unit). Discuss the Example with the students. The figure has been subdivided into unit squares where possible (six unit squares). The remaining part of the figure must be subdivided into two half-squares. Encourage students to use only vertical and horizontal subdivision lines. Although any of the six unit squares could be subdivided into half-squares, this is not necessary or practical. Suggest that students use half-squares only when necessary. Encourage them to verbalize the relationship between the three numbers in each solution. In the Example, the two half-squares equal one square unit. So, six squares plus one square equals an area of 7.

ANSWERS:

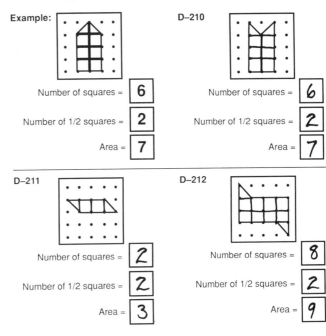

❑ PAGE 216: This page continues the activity from page 215, using more complex figures. Suggest again that students use half squares in the subdivision only when necessary, and encourage them to use only vertical and horizontal subdivision lines. Also, encourage students to verbalize the relationship between the three numbers in each solution. For example in D–214, four half-squares equal two unit squares. So, four squares plus two squares equals an area of 6.

ANSWERS:

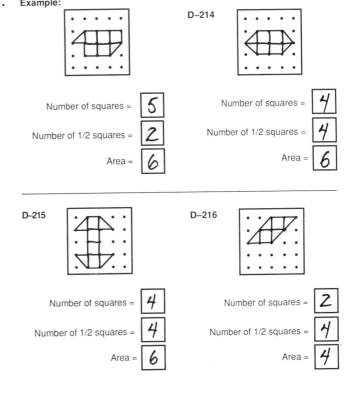

❑ **PAGE 217:** This activity introduces the task of constructing a figure on the geoboard design to match a given area. Note that several different figures could be drawn to match the given area. Suggest that students use only horizontal and vertical lines in their constructions. In the Example, discuss other possible solutions (a 2 x 2 square, an "L" shape, a "T" shape, etc.). If manipulatives (cubes or tiles) are available, have students experiment with different figures for a given area. Note that in D–218 a rectangle with area 7 cannot be formed on the geoboard (a 1 x 7 will not fit on the geoboard).

ANSWERS:

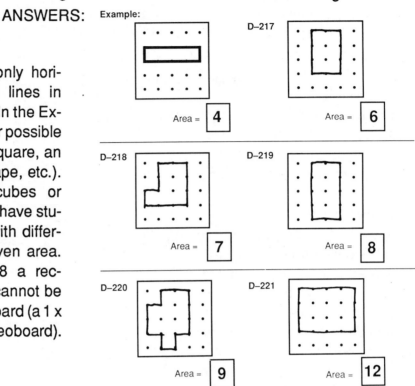

❑ **PAGE 218:** The activity from page 217 is extended here to more complex figures that involve half-units. Use the Example to discuss a possible strategy for solving these exercises. The top of the drawn figure contains two half-units, so completion of the figure requires six more unit squares. The simplest figure to satisfy this is pictured. Discuss other possible solutions with students. Geoboards or additional dot paper may be useful for experimentation. Only horizontal and vertical lines are necessary to solve all exercises except D–225. Note that in D–225 an additional one-half unit must be included in the figure, requiring a second diagonal line in the figure.

ANSWERS:

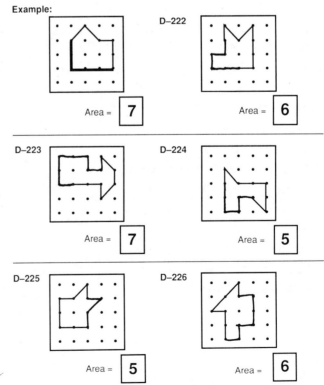

PAGES 219–220 ESTIMATING AREA

Mathematical Concepts
- Subdividing regions
- Estimating area
- Strategies for estimating area

VERBAL ANALYSIS STRATEGIES AND ANSWERS

❑ PAGE 219: These exercises introduce the concept of estimating area. Discuss with students strategies that use approximation rather than actual computation of area. One such strategy involves subdividing figures into unit squares, one-half squares, and other triangular regions. Discuss the Example with the students. Using the procedures from pages 215–216, the figure can be subdivided into squares (3) and one-half squares (6). In this case the area can be computed and is 6. However, using these procedures in the exercises will not subdivide the figures into squares and one-half squares. Triangles other than one-half squares will be formed. For the figure in D–227, subdivision may give two squares, two half-squares, and two right triangles (with legs of one and two units). Using just the squares and half squares, the area must be greater than 3. Thus 3 can be eliminated as a choice. Focus discussion on the area of the other right triangles. Since the area of each triangle is greater than 1/2, 1 can be used as an estimate of the area. Thus the area of the figure can be estimated to be 5. (Note: Each of these right triangles is one-half of a 1 x 2 rectangle, and thus has an area of exactly 1.) In exercises D–227 and D–228, each figure can be embedded in a 3 x 3 square. Thus the area of each figure must be less than nine units, and the choices 9 and 10 in these exercises can be eliminated.

ANSWERS: **D–227** [5]   **D–228** [5]   **D–229** [10]

❑ PAGE 220: The focus of this activity is on comparison of two figures with respect to area. With most figures pictured on this page, it is difficult or impossible to use the strategy of subdivision into squares and one-half squares. Discuss the following strategy for comparison: 1) place both figures on the same geoboard design overlapping as much as possible, and 2) compare the non-overlapping regions. In the Example, ask students to transfer the triangle on the left to the geoboard design on the right, and have them compare the non-overlapping regions. It should be visually apparent that the right triangle has the larger area. Note in the three exercises that one figure can always be embedded in the other figure being compared. Encourage students to estimate which figure has the larger area, then have them transfer the other figure for comparison.

ANSWERS: Example:

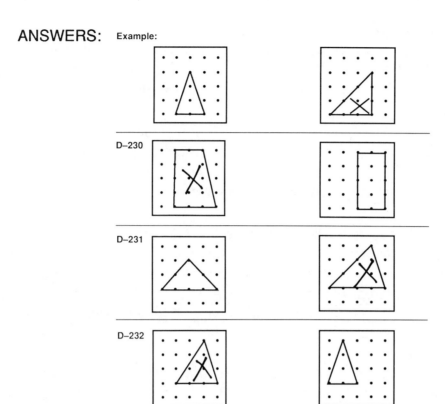

D–230

D–231

D–232

PAGES 221–222   AREA/DISTANCE AROUND

Mathematical Concepts
• Computing area (sums and products)
• Computing perimeter

VERBAL ANALYSIS STRATEGIES AND ANSWERS

❑   PAGE 221: This page introduces the activity of identifying a computation that can be used to compute the area (or perimeter) of a rectangle. Review with students earlier strategies for computing area (pages 203–204) and computing perimeter (pages 191–192). In the Example, ask students to identify what each computation might represent. For example, 4 + 2 + 4 + 2 = perimeter; 4 + 2 is the length of two sides, and 2 x 4 = area. The "3" and "5" in each other computation can be related to the number of dots and do not relate to length. After completing the exercises, ask students to identify what each other computation might represent.

ANSWERS: **D–233** [3 + 2 + 3 + 2]   **D–235** [2 + 2 + 2 + 2]
               D–234 [3 x 3]

❑   PAGE 222: More complex figures are used to extend the exercises from page 221. Review the computation of area and perimeter. Especially review area by summing, as introduced on pages 201–202. After completing the exercises, ask students to identify the computations for the perimeters in D–236 and D–238, and the computation for the area in D–237.

ANSWERS: **D–236** [3 + 3 + 2]
                D–237 [1 + 1 + 1 + 1 + 2 + 4 + 2 + 2]
                D–238 [4 + 4 + 2 + 2]

INTRODUCTION TO RELATIONS

The **Relations** section of **MATHEMATICAL REASONING** offers students the opportunity to use the reasoning skills developed in previous sections in analyzing and describing relationships between numbers. The activities encourage students to use a variety of mathematical ideas to describe these relations, including number magnitude, properties of numbers, and arithmetic operations.

This section uses three major mathematical ideas to explore these relations:

- order
- number patterns
- functions

Students are asked to use the order relations to compare numbers and expressions involving arithmetic operations, to order two or three numbers, and to construct number sentences. The activities involving number sentences include supplying missing numbers, missing operations, or missing order relations.

Several activities in this section use number sequences to focus student attention on discovering and describing number patterns. After describing the characteristics of these number patterns, students are then asked to identify a set of values that can be used to extend or complete a particular sequence. Number patterns are also used to explore properties of multiples and divisibility.

The relationship between pairs of numbers is introduced through the use of the function machine model. Functions presented in this section involve the four basic arithmetic operations, and activities focus on discovering a rule that describes a relationship between pairs of numbers. After determining the underlying relationship, students are asked to supply additional numbers that satisfy the function rule.

PAGES 223–224   COMPARING NUMBERS

Mathematical Concepts
- Comparing numbers (largest, smallest)
- Arithmetic facts (+, −, x, ÷)
- Strategies for ordering sets

VERBAL ANALYSIS STRATEGIES AND ANSWERS

❑   PAGE 223: Students are asked to identify the largest and smallest numbers in a set of whole numbers. Discuss two strategies with them: 1) comparing pairs of numbers in each set and using elimination until the largest number is determined, then repeating the process to find the smallest number; and 2) ordering the numbers in each set from smallest to largest using a number line, or forming an ordered list. After this process both the smallest and largest numbers in the set will be identified. Using the first strategy with the Example, compare 3 and 8; 8 is larger so compare 8 and 7 and so on until the largest number is found. This process can be repeated to find the smallest number. Using the second strategy, students may use the number-line model or slips of paper to place the numbers in their relative positions. Note that the solution to E–6 is the largest number in the set of circled answers, and the solution to E–7 is the smallest number in the set of underlined numbers.

ANSWERS: **E–1** [9, 1]   **E–4** [167, 93]   **E–7** [1]
          E–2 [23, 6]   **E–5** [482, 135]
          E–3 [27, 5]   **E–6** [482]

❑   PAGE 224: In this extension of the previous page students must perform the indicated arithmetic computations prior to locating the largest and smallest values in the set. After completing the computations, encourage students to employ one of the two strategies discussed on page 223. Note that the answer to E–13 is the largest of the circled values, and the answer to E–14 is the smallest of the underlined values.

ANSWERS: **E–8** [9 + 9, 6 + 2]   **E–12** [12 + 8, 30 ÷ 6]
          E–9 [17 − 3, 16 − 8]   **E–13** [49 + 7]
          E–10 [7 x 5, 9 + 6]   **E–14** [30 ÷ 6]
          E–11 [49 + 7, 42 ÷ 7]

PAGES 225–232   USING THE ORDER RELATIONS

Mathematical Concepts
- Order relations (<, >, =)
- Comparing numbers
- Arithmetic computation (+, −, x)
- Replacement set for inequalities
- True and false order relations

VERBAL ANALYSIS STRATEGIES AND ANSWERS

❑   PAGE 225: These exercises introduce the basic order relations (<, >, =) used in comparing or ordering numbers. Discuss the three order symbols and their uses, and relate them to relative position on the number line. In the Example, 12 < 13 indicates that 12 comes before 13 on the number line. After completing the exercises, discuss the relationship between "<" and ">" when comparing numbers. In the Example, 12 < 13 could be rewritten as 13 > 12 and read as "13 is greater than 12." Ask students to rewrite and verbalize the solutions to those exercises involving the symbols < and >.

ANSWERS: **E–15** [>]   **E–18** [>]   **E–21** [>]
             E–16 [<]   **E–19** [<]   **E–22** [=]
             E–17 [=]   **E–20** [=]   **E–23** [>]

❑   PAGE 226: The use of order relations is continued by asking students to select a number to complete an order relation. After completing the exercises, ask students to verbalize the completed order relation. In the Example, 16 < 17 is read "16 is less than 17." Also, ask students to use order relations to explain why the other two choices are not solutions. In the Example, "15 is less than 16, so it is not a solution," and "16 equals 16 and is not a solution."

ANSWERS: **E–24** [a. 46]   **E–29** [b. 9]
             E–25 [b. 23 + 22]   **E–30** [b. 15]
             E–26 [c. 16 + 18]   **E–31** [b. 9]
             E–27 [c. 15 + 14]   **E–32** [a. 13 + 13]
             E–28 [a. 6 x 7]

❑   PAGE 227: This page extends the previous activities to the comparison of three numbers by order relations. Students must identify all of the numbers from a replacement set that satisfy the given order relationships. Discuss with students the strategy of trying each number from the replacement in the circle, then determining whether the resulting relation is true. In the Example, ask students to verbalize why 10 and 14 are not solutions. In E–36 through E–39 stress the need to check both inequalities. For example, in E–36 the replacement number must satisfy the two relations: 1) 12 is greater than the replacement number, and 2) the replacement number is greater than 8. After completing the exercises, it may be helpful to discuss the order relationships in terms of numbers between two given numbers as was done for pages 45 and 46.

ANSWERS: **E–33** [25, 34]   **E–37** [19, 15]
             E–34 [19, 23, 6]   **E–38** [36]
             E–35 [8]   **E–39** [15, 20, 35]
             E–36 [11, 9]

❑ PAGE 228: The exercises from page 227 are extended here to placing three numbers in a given order relation. Discuss the Example with the students. The order relations are *greater than*, so the ordering of the given numbers must be from largest to smallest. Which exercise is similar to the Example? (E–44) Note that the relations in E–42 are *less than*, so ordering must be from smallest to largest. In exercises such as E–40, encourage students to fill in the two equal values first.

ANSWERS: **E–40** [3, 8, 8]   **E–44** [35, 21, 13]
             E–41 [5, 5, 17]   **E–45** [9, 7, 7]
             E–42 [8, 12, 16]   **E–46** [36, 40, 40]
             E–43 [11, 16, 23]

❑ PAGE 229: Students are asked to distinguish between true and false statements involving order relations. After completing the exercises, ask students how the false sentences in each exercise could be changed to make them true. In the Example, the false sentence 4 x 5 < 20 could be changed to either 4 x 5 = 20, or 4 x 5 < 21 (here 21 could be replaced by any other number greater than 20).

ANSWERS: **E–47** [6 x 5 > 25]   **E–51** [14 < 13 + 3]
             E–48 [9 + 8 > 15]   **E–52** [17 – 7 > 7]
             E–49 [18 – 7 < 18]   **E–53** [50 > 50 – 32]
             E–50 [16 + 12 = 28]

❑ PAGE 230: In this activity students are asked to form true sentences by supplying the correct order relation. After completing the arithmetic computations, encourage students to verbalize the relationship between the two numbers being compared, then select the correct order symbol. In the Example, 3 + 4 = 7, and 7 is less than 12. Thus, the correct symbol is "<." After completing the exercises, students might be asked to compare the sentences within exercises. For example, in E–54, since 5 + 6 = 11, then 5 plus any number greater than 6 must be greater than 11, implying that 5 + 7 > 11. Similarly, in E–58, since 8 + 19 = 27, then 19 + 7 must be less than 27, and 18 + 19 must be greater than 27.

ANSWERS:

Example:				E–54		
3 + 4	$<$	12		5 + 6	$=$	11
3 + 4	$>$	5		5 + 7	$>$	11
3 + 4	$=$	7		5 × 7	$>$	11

E–55				E–56		
9 × 9	$>$	18		4	$<$	12 – 6
9 + 9	$=$	18		7	$>$	12 – 6
9 – 9	$<$	18		5	$<$	12 – 6

E–57				E–58		
20	$=$	13 + 7		19 + 7	$<$	27
20	$=$	7 + 13		8 + 19	$=$	27
20	$>$	13 – 7		18 + 19	$>$	27

E–59				E–60		
23 + 23	$<$	60		90	$>$	43 + 43
37 + 15	$<$	60		90	$>$	43 × 2
15 × 4	$=$	60		90	$>$	43 – 43

❑   PAGE 231: On this page students must identify all numbers from a replacement set that will make a number sentence involving order relations true. Encourage students to use the strategy of trial and error introduced on page 227. Discuss the Example with the students. Ask them to explain why 3 and 5 are solutions but 1 and 2 are not. Similarly, ask students to explain why numbers in the replacement sets are (or are not) solutions to the exercises.

ANSWERS: **E–61** [9]   **E–64** [4, 8]   **E–67** [3, 4]
           E–62 [10, 8]   **E–65** [5]
           E–63 [0]   **E–66** [13, 10]

❑   PAGE 232: These exercises continue the activity on page 231. Discuss exercise E–68 with the students. Note that since 8 + 7 = 15, then all numbers less than 7 will make a sum less than 15 and make the sentence true. Thus 2, 3, and 6 should be circled. Likewise, any number greater than 7 will make a sum greater than 15 and make the sentence false. In E–69, since 7 x 9 = 63, only numbers greater than 63 should be circled.

ANSWERS: **E–68** [2, 3, 6]   **E–72** [7]
           E–69 [73, 83]   **E–73** [10, 12, 16]
           E–70 [2, 3]   **E–74** [17, 19]
           E–71 [0, 2]   **E–75** [6, 16, 24]

PAGES 233–236   NUMBER SENTENCES

Mathematical Concepts
• Order relations (>, <, =)
• Comparing numbers
• Arithmetic computation (+, –, x, ÷)
• Number sentences
• Ordered pairs of numbers

VERBAL ANALYSIS STRATEGIES AND ANSWERS

❑   PAGE 233: To complete this activity students are asked to select an operation that will make a true number sentence. In each exercise there is a unique solution. Discuss the Example with the students. Ask them to substitute each operation in the number sentence and discuss the results. For example, substituting "x" in the sentence will make 9 x 8 = 17, which is false. How could this multiplication sentence be made true? (Either change 17 to 72 or change the = symbol to >.) Ask students to complete the exercises by substituting each operation and determining whether the sentence is true. After completing the exercises, discuss why the uncircled choices do not make true sentences. How could these false sentences be changed to make the sentences true?

ANSWERS: **E–76** [–]   **E–79** [÷]   **E–82** [÷]
          E–77 [X]   **E–80** [–]
          E–78 [X]   **E–81** [÷]

❑   PAGE 234: This page continues the activity from page 233. Since some exercises can be made true by using more than one operation, encourage students to substitute *each* of the four operations in the sentence. (Note that E–84, E–85, and E–86 have multiple solutions, even though students are asked to find only one correct operation.) After completing the exercises, ask students to compare answers to determine all possible solutions. As on page 233, discuss why some operations do not make true sentences.

ANSWERS: **E–83** [X]   **E–86** [+, X]   **E–89** [–]
          E–84 [+, X]   **E–87** [÷]   **E–90** [X]
          E–85 [+, –, X] **E–88** [÷]   **E–91** [X]

❑   PAGE 235: Introduced here is the task of using ordered pairs of numbers to make true sentences. Discuss the Example with the students. Stress the concept of *ordered pair* by making sure students place the first given number in the box and the second in the circle. Reversing the order affects the solutions in E–94 and E–95 (subtraction and division are not commutative). Note that 17, 8 is a solution to E–94, but 8, 17 is not. Stress that all ordered pairs should be substituted into each sentence, since some exercises have more than one solution. After completing the exercises, discuss why the uncircled choices do not make true sentences, and how they could be changed to make them true.

ANSWERS: **E–92** [b. 8, 9   c. 9, 9]   **E–95** [b. 63, 7]
             E–93 [a. 6, 7   b. 6, 6]   **E–96** [a. 7, 7]
             E–94 [d. 17, 8]

❑   PAGE 236: In this extension of the activity from page 235, stress again the importance of order, and make sure students place the first number of each pair in the box and the second number in the circle. In the Example, discuss the effect of reversing the box number and circle number. The solution (c. 3, 5) would become the ordered pair 5, 3 and would no longer be a solution to the bottom sentence. Would it be a solution to the top sentence? (Yes.) After completing the exercises, discuss with students the effect on sentences of reversing the ordered pairs.

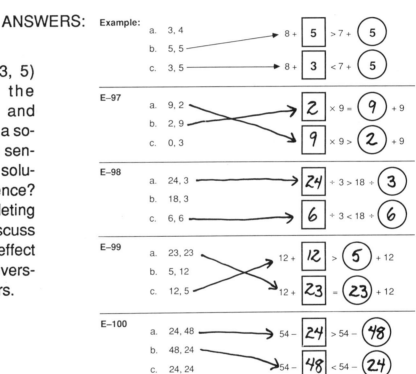

PAGES 237–240   SEQUENCES OF NUMBERS

Mathematical Concepts
- Sequences of numbers
- Number patterns
- Properties of sets of numbers
- Extending sequences
- Sequences on the number line

VERBAL ANALYSIS STRATEGIES AND ANSWERS

❏   PAGE 237: This activity asks students to extend a sequence of numbers by identifying a pattern or relationship between the given numbers in that sequence. Discuss the following strategy with students: 1) examine the given sequence to discover patterns or properties of the numbers in the sequence; 2) examine each of the choices (a., b., and c.) to see if they have the same pattern or properties; and 3) make sure the choice is a continuation of the given sequence (that is, the choices do not overlap or leave a gap in the sequence). Discuss the Example with the students. Students may identify a pattern (a difference of two between numbers) or discover a property (consecutive odd numbers). Discuss choices a. through c. with respect to these strategies. Choice a. does not have a difference of two or represent consecutive odd numbers. Choice b. has a difference of two and has consecutive odd numbers, but it overlaps (the 9 is repeated). Finally, choice c. satisfies both criteria *and* is a continuation of the given sequence, and thus is the solution. As students complete the exercises, encourage them to write their choice at the end of the given sequence. This will insure that the last number in the given sequence and first number in their choice satisfies the pattern.

ANSWERS: **E–101** [b. 16, 19, 22, 25]   **E–103** [c. 25, 20, 15, 10]
                  E–102 [a. 1, 5, 1, 6]   **E–104** [c. 10, 9, 12, 11]

❏   PAGE 238: These activities are similar to those on page 237, but ask students to identify the beginning of a given sequence. Again, discuss the strategy outlined on page 237. Discuss the Example with the students. The numbers in the given sequence differ by two and are consecutive even numbers. Stress that the solution must *precede* the given sequence. Choice a. fits the patterns above but comes after, not before, the given sequence, and choice c. overlaps the given sequence. Encourage students to write their choices at the beginning of the given sequence when they check their patterns or properties.

ANSWERS: **E–105** [c. 1, 5, 9, 13]   **E–107** [b. 40, 35, 30, 25]
                  E–106 [a. 6, 9, 12, 15]   **E–108** [c. 2, 5, 8, 11]

❏   PAGE 239: In this activity students must fill in missing values in a sequence. These missing values may appear at the beginning, end, or in the middle of the sequence. Continue to focus on determining patterns or properties of the given numbers in the sequence. Locating the given numbers on a number line may help students discover patterns or properties for the sequences. In the Example, the following patterns or properties may be discussed: 1) numbers differ by three, 2) all are consecutive multiples of 3, and 3) there are three units between each successive number on the number line. Discuss completing the sequence using each of these observations.

ANSWERS: **E–109** [14, 19, 34]   **E–113** [10, 13, 16]
E–110 [21, 19, 17]   **E–114** [38, 35, 23, 20]
E–111 [35, 40, 60, 65]   **E–115** [9, 15, 21, 27]
E–112 [2, 6, 8]

❑ PAGE 240: These exercises require that students identify a portion of a sequence that is not an immediate continuation of the given sequence. The three-dot notation suggests a gap in the sequence. Recommend that students use the previous strategy to identify patterns, use these patterns to continue the sequence until they reach the largest beginning number in the three choices, then verify that the pattern continues in the selected choice. Again, the use of a number line may help to extend the sequence. In the Example, if the pattern is viewed as consecutive multiples of 3, the sequence can be extended as follows: 3, 6, 9, 12, 15, 18, 21, 24, 27, **30**…. Note that 18 is in this sequence, but not all numbers in choice a. are multiples of 3. Also, no values in choice b. are multiples of 3. Choice c. connects with the sequence and consists of consecutive multiples of 3.

ANSWERS: **E–116** [a. 55, 60, 65, 70]   **E–118** [c. 30, 32, 34, 36]
E–117 [c. 19, 21, 23, 25]   **E–119** [a. 34, 39, 44, 49]

PAGES 241–248   USING NUMBER MACHINES/ PAIRING NUMBERS

Mathematical Concepts
- Functions (number-machine model)
- Sequences of numbers
- Describing a function in terms of an arithmetic operation
- Functions as number pairs
- Constant function
- Functions involving two arithmetic operations

VERBAL ANALYSIS STRATEGIES AND ANSWERS

❑ PAGE 241: The number machine model is used to introduce the function concept. The exercises focus on determining a relationship between pairs of numbers (those going into a machine and those coming out). Ask students to verbalize this relationship in terms of "what the machine in each exercise does to the numbers." In the Example, verbalizations may include: "makes a number two bigger," "adds two to each number in the box," or "makes the next bigger odd or even number." After completing the exercises, discuss with students the properties of the sequence of numbers in the boxes and the sequence of numbers in the circles. However, determining solutions to these exercises based on the circled sequences will only work when the boxed numbers are consecutive counting numbers. This method will not always work in activities on later pages.

ANSWERS: **E–120** [9]   **E–121** [8]

❏ PAGE 242: This page continues the activity from page 241. Encourage students again to verbalize the relationship between the boxed numbers and the circled numbers. Ask students to explain this relationship in terms of arithmetic operations. For example, in E–122 "each boxed number is multiplied by 3." Since the boxed numbers are consecutive counting numbers, the exercises can be solved by completing the sequences pictured in the circles, but this method will not always work on later pages.

ANSWERS: **E–122** [9]   **E–123** [4]   **E–124** [3]

❏ PAGE 243: These exercises emphasize the concept of a function. In each exercise one circled number does not follow the rule for the function. The student must identify a rule that will work in three of the four pictured machines. Discuss the Example with the students. What does the machine do to 5? (It adds 3.) What does the machine do to 6? (It adds 4.) What does the machine do to 7 (It also adds 4.) What does the rule for the machine seem to be? (It adds 4 to the number.) Verify if this works by checking what the machine does to 8. After completing the exercises, ask students what numbers should replace the numbers with X's. Note in these exercises that using the circled sequence does not provide an obvious solution.

ANSWERS: **E–125** [X on 9]   **E–126** [X on 13]

❏ PAGE 244: In this continuation of page 243, again focus attention on determining the arithmetic operation that defines the function. In E–127 the function "subtracts 3," and in E–128 it "multiplies by 3." Exercise E–129 requires two operations to describe the function ("multiply by 2, then add 1"). Students may have difficulty finding a rule for this exercise. If students focus on addition alone, they may use the pattern 15 + **16** = 31, 16 + **17** = 33, 17 + **17** = 34 to conclude that the rule is to "add 17." But this rule is not verified by the last machine, since 18 + **17** ≠ 37. Remind students that only one circled number is incorrect.

ANSWERS: **E–127** [X on 2]   **E–128** [X on 16]   **E–129** [X on 34]

❑ PAGE 245: The first three boxed numbers in these exercises are consecutive, and the three-dot notation indicates that several machines are not pictured. Students must determine a rule based on the first three machines and apply this rule to the last machine. Discuss the Example with the students and ask them to verbalize the rule as an operation (box number plus 1). What is the circled number in the last machine? (9 + **1** = 10) Ask students to fill in the missing machines (indicated by the dots) to verify the solution. Encourage students to verbalize the rule for each exercise in terms of an arithmetic operation. (In E–130 "add 3," and in E–131 "subtract one.") Filling in the missing machines may not be feasible in these exercises (E–130 has 13 missing, and E–131 has 8 missing).

ANSWERS: **E–130** [20]   **E–131** [7]

❑ PAGE 246: These exercises continue those on page 245. In E–132 and E–134 the boxed numbers are not consecutive. Have students focus on the rule in terms of operations. (In E–132 "add 8," and in E–133 "add 4.") Note that the rule for E–134 requires two operations ("multiply by 2, then add 1.")

ANSWERS: **E–132** [22]   **E–133** [10]   **E–134** [35]

❑ PAGE 247: This page is an extension of the previous function activities, but the number-machine model is replaced by an arrow. Also, numbers in the top row are not written in consecutive order. Discuss the Example with the students. Encourage them to describe the pairing in terms of an arithmetic operation. What is done to the top number to get the bottom number? ("Subtract 1.") Using this rule, what are the missing values? Exercises E–135, E–137, and E–138 can be described by single arithmetic operations. ("Multiply by 2," "add 5," and "subtract 3.") No single operation describes the pairings in exercise E–136. What is true about the pairing in the first four sets of numbers? (The result is always 5.) Use this observation as a rule to complete the exercise.

ANSWERS: **E–135** [14, 18, 20]   **E–137** [6, 17, 13]
         E–136 [5, 5, 5]   **E–138** [11, 3, 0]

❑ PAGE 248: As a continuation of page 247, encourage students to describe the pair relationship as an arithmetic operation where possible. (E–139 is "multiply by 3," E–141 is "add 10," and E–143 is "subtract 2.") No single operation describes the pairings in E–140 and E–142. The pairing in E–140 can be described as either "even numbers pair with 0, odd numbers pair with 1" or as "multiply even numbers by 0, divide each odd number by itself." Also, every number in E–142 is paired with the number 2 (similar to exercise E–136 on page 247).

ANSWERS: **E–139** [18, 12, 27]   **E–142** [2, 2, 2]
          E–140 [0, 1, 0]   **E–143** [3, 7, 2]
          E–141 [12, 22, 18]

PAGES 249–250   MULTIPLES OF 2, 3, AND 5

Mathematical Concepts
- Multiples of 2, 3, and 5
- Common multiples
- Counting using multiples
- Patterns to identify multiples (2, 5)

VERBAL ANALYSIS STRATEGIES AND ANSWERS

❑ PAGE 249: The classification of numbers using the concept of multiples (2, 3, and 5) is introduced here. Review with students the concept of multiples and counting in multiples (of 2, 3, and 5) from pages 19–20. After completing the initial activity, discuss E–144 with the students. How can the solution to E–144 be identified in terms of the numbers in the circles, squares and triangles? (Multiples common to 2 and 3 must appear in both a circle and a square.) Similarly discuss the characteristics of the common multiples in E–145 through E–147. When the exercises are complete, discuss the visual patterns formed by multiples in the rectangle. (Multiples of 2 appear on diagonal lines, and multiples of 3 appear on other diagonal lines. All multiples of 5 appear in the last column.)

ANSWERS:

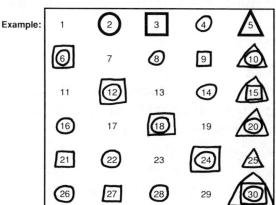

E–144 Which multiples of 2 are also multiples of 3? **6, 12, 18, 24, 30**

E–145 Which multiples of 2 are also multiples of 5? **10, 20, 30**

E–146 Which multiples of 3 are also multiples of 5? **15, 30**

E–147 Which numbers are multiples of all three numbers? **30**

❑ PAGE 250: Students are asked to identify multiples of 2, 3, and 5 in a given set of numbers. Use the Example to discuss several strategies for solving the exercises: 1) each multiple of 2 must be the answer to a multiplication problem with a factor of 2 ($12 = 2 \times 6$, $18 = 2 \times 9$, $24 = 2 \times 12$...); 2) a list of multiples of 2 can be written and used for comparison; or 3) focus on patterns such as all multiples of 2 that have the digit 0, 2, 4, 6, or 8 in the units place. A pattern that could be used in E–149 is "all multiples of 5 have a 0 or 5 in the units place."

ANSWERS: **E–148** [9, 3, 12, 6, 15, 18]
           E–149 [15, 10, 50, 35]
           E–150 [22, 10, 8, 12, 2 , 6, 18]

PAGES 251–252   DIVIDING USING 2, 3, AND 5

Mathematical Concepts
- Divisibility by 2, 3, and 5
- Multiples of 2, 3, and 5
- Division by 2, 3, and 5
- Remainders

VERBAL ANALYSIS STRATEGIES AND ANSWERS

❑ PAGE 251: In these exercises students are asked to identify numbers that are divisible by 2, 3, and 5. In terms of the operation of division, *divisibility* means "leaves a remainder of zero." Use the Example to discuss the strategies that were outlined on page 250: using multiplication facts for 3, making a list of multiples of 3, and focusing on patterns (for 2 and 5) in the exercises. If students have a basic knowledge of division, dividing by 2, 3, and 5 provides an alternate strategy for determining the solutions. If the division strategy is used in the Example, why are 8 and 11 not divisible by 3? (They each leave a remainder of 2.)

ANSWERS: **E–151** [10, 6, 20]   **E–154** [30, 12, 10]
           E–152 [15, 10]   **E–155** [30, 25, 5, 10]
           E–153 [6, 3, 15]

❑ PAGE 252: This activity focuses on the division strategy from page 251. This strategy is used to identify numbers that leave a specific remainder when dividing by 2, 3, or 5. Discuss the Example with the students, emphasizing the division strategy. Which numbers are divisible by 2? (8, 10, and 6.) Explain why they are divisible by 2. (Each leaves a remainder of zero.) Explain why 7 and 5 are solutions to the Example. After completing the exercises, ask students to consider the solutions to the Example and to E–158. How can the circled values be described? (They are all odd numbers.) Ask students to compare E–156 to E–157. Why is 12 not circled in either exercise? (It leaves a remainder of zero.) Also, ask students to discuss the remainders of the uncircled numbers in E–159 and E–160.

ANSWERS: **E–156** [7, 10]   **E–159** [6, 11]
                  E–157 [11, 8]   **E–160** [17]
                  E–158 [11, 9, 3]

PAGES 253–254   BASIC FACTS USING 1, 2, 3 AND 5

Mathematical Concepts
- Permutations of two numbers
- Addition facts
- Multiplication facts
- Commutativity (+ and x)

VERBAL ANALYSIS STRATEGIES AND ANSWERS

❑   PAGE 253: Students must identify all possible addition facts that can be made using 1, 2, or 3 as addends. Encourage students to fill in all the boxes (using 1, 2, or 3) before completing the sums. After completing the exercises, ask students to compare solutions to verify that all the possible facts have been formed. A strategy that can be used to systematically determine all possible facts is writing all possible pairs with 1 as the first addend (1 + 1, 1 + 2, 1 + 3), then all pairs with 2 as the first addend, and then all pairs beginning with 3. After completing the exercises, ask students to identify exercises that have the same circled value. Compare these sums in terms of commutativity.

ANSWERS: Example:

$\boxed{2} + \boxed{3} = \boxed{5}$

E–161 $\boxed{1} + \boxed{1} = \boxed{2}$ E–162 $\boxed{3} + \boxed{3} = \boxed{6}$

E–163 $\boxed{1} + \boxed{2} = \boxed{3}$ E–164 $\boxed{2} + \boxed{1} = \boxed{3}$

E–165 $\boxed{1} + \boxed{3} = \boxed{4}$ E–166 $\boxed{3} + \boxed{1} = \boxed{4}$

E–167 $\boxed{2} + \boxed{2} = \boxed{4}$ E–168 $\boxed{3} + \boxed{2} = \boxed{5}$

❑   PAGE 254: These exercises parallel those on page 253, using the operation of multiplication and the numbers 2, 3, and 5. Suggest that students follow the strategy outlined on page 253. After completing the exercises, compare products in terms of commutativity.

ANSWERS: Example: $\boxed{5} \times \boxed{3} = \bigcirc{15}$

E–169   E–170

$\boxed{2} \times \boxed{2} = \bigcirc{4}$ $\boxed{3} \times \boxed{2} = \bigcirc{6}$

E–171   E–172

$\boxed{2} \times \boxed{3} = \bigcirc{6}$ $\boxed{5} \times \boxed{2} = \bigcirc{10}$

E–173   E–174

$\boxed{2} \times \boxed{5} = \bigcirc{10}$ $\boxed{3} \times \boxed{5} = \bigcirc{15}$

E–175   E–176

$\boxed{3} \times \boxed{3} = \bigcirc{9}$ $\boxed{5} \times \boxed{5} = \bigcirc{25}$

INTRODUCTION TO TABLES AND GRAPHS

The **Tables and Graphs** section of **MATHEMATICAL REASONING** introduces students to the mathematical principles that serve as the foundation for the development and use of tables, charts, and graphs. The activities focus on the tasks of assembling, organizing, and interpreting data and presenting data in different formats.

This section emphasizes two major themes:

- organizing and displaying data in tables, charts, and graphs
- using data from tables, charts, and graphs to solve a variety of word problems

The initial activities introduce students to the task of reading and analyzing tables, charts, or graphs using given data. After the students are able to analyze and describe data in these formats, they are presented with word problems whose solutions require the use of data from tables, charts, or graphs. Finally, students are asked to examine and compare the relationships between tables and graphs constructed from the same data.

This section also introduces students to the use of a letter-number coordinate system as a means of locating and identifying rectangular regions within a chart. Later activities extend this concept to the task of locating and describing points on a rectangular coordinate system (letter-number). These activities serve to lay the groundwork for understanding the Cartesian Coordinate System.

PAGES 255–260   READING AND MAKING TABLES

Mathematical Concepts
- Reading tables
- Solving word problems using tables
- Recording data in a table

VERBAL ANALYSIS STRATEGIES AND ANSWERS

❑   PAGE 255: This page introduces a series of activities using tabular data. These activities require students to examine a given table and use the data to solve simple word problems. Before beginning the first exercises, discuss the table and focus on verbalizing the information. For example (relating the left column to the right column), "On Monday 35 students were absent"; and (relating the right column to the left column) "19 students were absent on Thursday." After completing the exercises, ask students how the data in the table was used to solve each exercise. For example, in F–3 the solution requires students to identify the smallest number in the right column.

ANSWERS: **F–1** [30]   **F–4** [125]
             F–2 [Tuesday]   **F–5** [Monday]
             F–3 [Wednesday]   **F–6** [Wednesday]

❑   PAGE 256: Here the table is more complex than the table on page 255. As on that page, discuss the table and focus on verbalizing the information. For example (relating the left column to the right columns), "Hope Street is two miles from Taylor School and one mile from City Park"; and (relating the right columns to the left column) "Taylor School and Hope Theater are both two miles from Elm Street." Discuss the meaning of zero in the first line of the table. (Hope Theater must be on Hope Street.) After completing the exercises, discuss how the data in the table was used to solve each exercise.

ANSWERS: **F–7** [1]   **F–10** [2]   **F–13** [Main]
             F–8 [4]   **F–11** [Main]   **F–14** [Town Hall]
             F–9 [2]   **F–12** [Park]

❑   PAGE 257: These exercises introduce the task of entering a set of data into a table. After entering the data, students are asked to use the table to solve simple word problems. Discuss the table, verifying that the information has been correctly entered. When the exercises are complete, discuss how the table was used to solve each exercise. For example, the solution to F–20 is the sum of all the numbers in the right column.

ANSWERS: **F–15** [11]   **F–18** [4]   **F–21** [4]
              F–16 [6]   **F–19** [Karen]   **F–22** [5]
              F–17 [4]   **F–20** [29]   **F–23** [Elaine]

❏   PAGE 258: Students must enter data into a more complex table. Discuss the two pieces of data (20 and 16) which appear in the Example. Ask students to locate this data in the sentences at the top of the page. Encourage them to record the data for Mr. Dodd's class first, then enter the data for Ms. Gilman's class. After students have entered the data, have them verify that the data is correctly entered before answering the word problems. When the exercises are complete, discuss how the table was used to solve each exercise. For example, in F–28 the solution requires students to sum two numbers from different columns (19 + 20). In F–30 students must sum all the numbers in the last column.

ANSWERS: **F–24** [23, 19]   **F–27** [21, 17]   **F–30** [93]
              F–25 [19, 20]   **F–28** [39]   **F–31** [Thursday]
              F–26 [24, 21]   **F–29** [38]   **F–32** [Monday]

❏   PAGE 259: The task of recording data in a table and solving word problems continues on this page. Discuss the entry of the three pieces of data (1, 2, 3) for Amy. For example, the 1 must be recorded in the last column under "school," and so on. After completing the data entry, have students verify that the data has been correctly entered by asking them to verbalize the data in each row. Then discuss how the table was used to solve each exercise.

ANSWERS: **F–33** [2, 3, 1]   **F–38** [3 miles]
              F–34 [1, 3, 4]   **F–39** [1 mile]
              F–35 [5, 1, 1]   **F–40** [Amy]
              F–36 [Elaine]   **F–41** [John]
              F–37 [Amy and John]

❏   PAGE 260: This activity continues the task from page 259, but the word problems are more complex. Solutions require combining or comparing up to four of the six pieces of data in the table. Note that in F–49 students riding to school would include both bus and car entries from the table. Thus, there are 16 + 5 = 21 riders in Mr. Dodd's class and 14 + 8 = 22 in Ms. Gilman's. This makes a total of 43. Also, F–50 requires students to compare the number of riders in each class.

ANSWERS: **F–42** [16, 14]   **F–45** [30]   **F–48** [29]
              F–43 [5, 8]   **F–46** [Mr. Dodd's]   **F–49** [43]
              F–44 [8, 6]   **F–47** [28]   **F–50** [Ms. Gilman's]

PAGES 261–266 READING AND MAKING BAR GRAPHS

Mathematical Concepts
- Reading bar graphs
- Solving word problems using graphs
- Recording data in a bar graph

VERBAL ANALYSIS STRATEGIES AND ANSWERS

❑ PAGE 261: This page introduces a series of activities using data recorded in a bar graph. These activities require students to interpret data in a bar graph and solve simple word problems. Before beginning the first exercises, discuss the graph and focus on verbalizing the information. For example (relating the horizontal labels to the vertical scale), "On Monday the high temperature was 40 degrees"; and (relating the vertical scale to the horizontal labels) "A high temperature of 50 degrees was recorded on Tuesday." After completing the exercises, discuss how the graph was used to solve each exercise. For example, to find a solution in F–52, students may locate 35 on the vertical scale and move horizontally until they find a bar of that height, which occurs on Wednesday.

ANSWERS: **F–51** [50° F]   **F–54** [beginning]
          F–52 [Wednesday]   **F–55** [Thursday, Sunday]
          F–53 [Friday]

❑ PAGE 262: The data on this page is represented by horizontal bars rather than vertical bars. As in the previous activity, discuss the graph and focus on verbalizing the information. For example (relating the vertical labels to the horizontal scale), "Amy slept 10 hours"; and (relating the horizontal scale to the vertical labels) "Eight hours of sleep was recorded for Peter." After completing the exercises, discuss how the graph was used in each solution. In F–60 some students may find the length of each bar and compute the difference ($11 - 7 = 4$), while other students may visually compare the two bars and conclude that Karen's is four units (hours) longer than John's.

ANSWERS: **F–56** [Karen]   **F–59** [Amy, Carla]
          F–57 [John]   **F–60** [4 hours]
          F–58 [Elaine]

❑ PAGE 263: These exercises introduce the task of using a table of data to complete the construction of a bar graph. Before entering data into the bar graph, discuss the table of data with students as on page 255. Also, ask students to relate the three bars pictured in the graph to the data in the table. After completing the bar graph, verify that the graph is drawn correctly by asking students to interpret the graph verbally. For example, "On June 22 the height is 6 cm." Have students compare the graph data to the data in the original table. This bar graph will also be used for the exercises on page 264.

ANSWERS:

Date	Height in Cm
June 1	2
June 8	2
June 15	4
June 22	6
June 29	10
July 6	16
July 13	18

Use the table to complete the following graph.

F–61

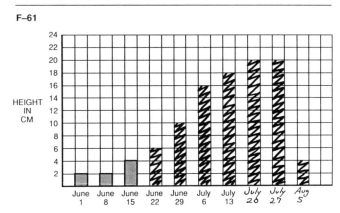

□ PAGE 264: Students are asked to add three bars to the graph from page 263, using additional given data, then to use the completed graph to solve word problems. Before beginning the exercises, discuss the horizontal scale with the students. What height was recorded on June 15? (4 cm) What height was recorded on June 22? (6 cm) How many days are there between June 15 and June 22? (7 days, or 1 week.) How much did the plant grow in that week? (2 cm) After completing the exercises, ask students to explain how they used the graph to solve each exercise.

ANSWERS: F–62 [10 cm]   F–67 [It stayed the same height.]
          F–63 [July 13]   F–68 [June 29–July 6]
          F–64 [16 cm]   F–69 [July 20–July 27]
          F–65 [6 cm]   F–70 [Maybe it was cut or died.]
          F–66 [6 cm]

❑ PAGE 265: This activity continues the task of using recorded data to complete a bar graph and solve word problems. Discuss how the given bar in the graph is related to the recorded data. Ask students to compare the list of names in the recorded data to the names on the horizontal scale in the graph (note that in the graph they are in alphabetical order). After students complete the graph, have them verify the data in the graph and answer the exercises. Have them explain how the graph was used to solve each exercise.

ANSWERS:

Ann   ✓✓✓✓✓✓✓
Carla ✓✓✓✓✓
Edward ✓✓✓✓✓✓✓✓✓
Brian ✓✓✓✓✓✓
Doug ✓✓✓✓

Use the results to complete the following bar graph.

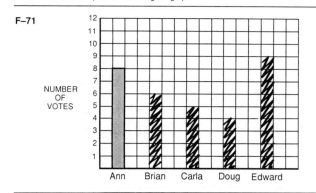

F–71

NUMBER OF VOTES

F–72 How many votes did Brian get?_____**6**_____

F–73 Who won the election?____**EDWARD**____

F–74 What was the total number of votes?____**32**____

❑ PAGE 266: The table of data here is more complex than previous tables. Discuss the table and focus on verbalizing the information. Ask students to relate the two given bars in the graph to the first line in the table. As students complete the bar graph, they may find it helpful to use a straightedge to line up the end of a bar with the correct value on the horizontal scale. When they have finished the graph, have students verify the data. After completing F–76 and F–77, discuss how the graph was used to find the answers (longest bar, shortest bar). Also discuss how the table could be used to solve the exercises. Which method of solution seems easier?

ANSWERS:

Day	TEMPERATURE IN FAHRENHEIT	
	High	Low
Monday	72	52
Tuesday	68	48
Wednesday	70	50
Thursday	74	52
Friday	76	56
Saturday	78	60
Sunday	80	68

Use the table to complete the following bar graph.

F–75

Day   TEMPERATURE IN FAHRENHEIT

Mon	Hi / Lo
Tues	Hi / Lo
Wed	Hi / Lo
Thur	Hi / Lo
Fri	Hi / Lo
Sat	Hi / Lo
Sun	Hi / Lo

0 4 8 12 16 20 24 28 32 36 40 44 48 52 56 60 64 68 72 76 80

F–76 What was the highest temperature for the week?____**80° F**____

F–77 What was the lowest temperature for the week?____**48° F**____

PAGES 267–274 READING CHARTS

Mathematical Concepts
- Rectangular coordinate system (letter-number)
- Given a position, name the coordinates
- Given the coordinates, locate a position
- Solving problems using a coordinate system

VERBAL ANALYSIS STRATEGIES AND ANSWERS

❑ PAGE 267: This begins a series of four activities that use a seating chart and relate positions in the chart to a letter-number coordinate system. Before beginning the exercises, discuss the layout of the seating chart. For example, describe row D (Linda, Harry, empty seat, Gerry). Referring to the Example, ask students to locate Sara's name in the seating chart. In what row is Sara? (C) In what chair is she seated? (4) Name her location. (C4) Ask which students are seated in F3 and A1. (Debbie and Andy.) After completing the exercises, ask students to identify the person seated in the uncircled locations in each exercise.

ANSWERS: **F–78** [E3]   **F–80** [B3]   **F–82** [F2]
F–79 [D1]   **F–81** [C2]

❑ PAGE 268: This page extends the activity from page 267. Students are asked to write the coordinates of various locations in the seating chart. Discuss the Example with the students. Ask them to locate Elise's name in the chart. What is her row? (E) What is her seat? (3) Stress that when writing coordinates, the row is written first. Thus, her coordinate position is written E3. After completing the exercises, discuss how the chart was used to solve the exercises. For example, in F–89 Cindy is seated between Harry and Hector. Cindy is in row E and seat 2, so her coordinate position is E2.

ANSWERS: **F–83** [F3]   **F–88** [A4, B2, D3, E4, F1, F4]
F–84 [C2]   **F–89** [E2]
F–85 [A3]   **F–90** [B1]
F–86 [D4]   **F–91** [A2, A1]
F–87 [B1]

❑ PAGE 269: The tasks from pages 267–268 are reversed in these exercises. Students are given the coordinates of a position and asked to locate that position in the seating chart. Discuss the first entry in the box in each exercise. The circled name in the chart corresponds to the coordinates C2 in exercise F–92. Similarly, the X and the √ in the chart match the entries C1 in F–93 and C3 in F–94. Students may use two strategies to solve F–95. They may locate the seat in the chart corresponding to each coordinate in the box, or they may determine the coordinates of the empty seats in the chart and compare them to the entries in the box.

ANSWERS:

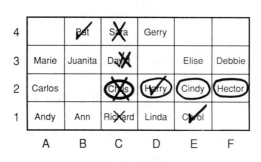

	A	B	C	D	E	F
4		Pat	Sara	Gerry		
3	Marie	Juanita	David		Elise	Debbie
2	Carlos		Chris	Harry	Cindy	Hector
1	Andy	Ann	Richard	Linda	Carol	

Circle the names of the people seated in the locations in the box.

F–92   C2, E2, D2, F2

Put an X on the names of the people seated in the locations in the box.

F–93   C1, C3, C4, C2

Put a √ on the names of the people seated in the locations in the box.

F–94   C3, E1, B4, D2

Circle the locations in the list below that are empty seats.

F–95   B2, C2, D3, A2, E3, A4, F1, F2

❏ PAGE 270: As an extension of page 269 students are given the coordinates of a location and asked to write the name of the person in that location. Use the Example to review with students the process of locating a position corresponding to a given coordinate. After completing the exercises, ask students to explain how they used the chart to solve exercises F–101 through F–104.

ANSWERS: **F–96**   [David]   **F–101** [Harry]
           F–97   [Pat]   **F–102** [Juanita]
           F–98   [Hector]   **F–103** [Cindy, Elise]
           F–99   [Carlos]   **F–104** [Juanita, Ann]
           F–100 [Ann]

❏ PAGE 271: This page begins a series of four activities using a 4 x 4 matrix of shapes to relate positions in a matrix to a letter-number coordinate system. Before beginning the first exercises, discuss the layout of the matrix. Note that in these exercises letters are used to identify columns, and numbers are used to identify rows. For example, in what column is the circle located? (A) In what row is the circle located? (4) Stress the order for writing the coordinates (column first, row second). List the coordinates of the circle. (A4) After completing the exercises, verify that students have located shapes congruent to the given figures and have recorded the correct coordinates.

ANSWERS: **F–105** [A1]   **F–108** [D4]   **F–110** [B4]
            F–106 [C2]   **F–109** [C3]   **F–111** [B2]
            F–107 [D1]

❏   PAGE 272: These exercises reverse the task on page 271. Students are given the coordinates of a position in the matrix and asked to draw the figure located in that position. Discuss the Example with the students. Locate and describe the figures in column B. In column B, locate and describe the figure in row 3. (This figure is a rectangle and is drawn in the Example.) After completing the exercises, verify the solutions by asking students to describe the properties of the figures drawn. For example, the figure in F–117 has five sides and two square corners.

ANSWERS:

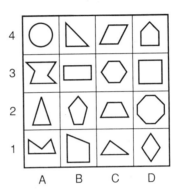

Draw the figures from the chart above next to their locations given below.

Example: B 3 _____   F–112 D 3 _____

F–113 A 2 _____   F–114 C 2 _____

F–115 A 4 _____   F–116 C 4 _____

F–117 D 4 _____   F–118 B 1 _____

❏   PAGE 273: Students are asked to locate three figures in the matrix given the coordinates of their positions, then to match the properties of these three figures with a written description. Prior to beginning the exercises, ask students to describe each figure in the matrix in terms of "number of sides" and "number of square corners." Discuss the Example with the students. Ask them to locate the three shapes and to verbalize their common property or properties. (Each figure has five sides.) Work with the students to locate and describe the properties of each set of figures in the exercises.

ANSWERS: **F–119** [e. Figures with more than four sides]
            F–120 [a. Triangles]
            F–121 [b. Figures with four sides]
            F–122 [c. Figures with one or more square corners]

❑   PAGE 274: Using the same matrix of shapes, students are asked to solve problems involving relational terms (between, below, above). Discuss the Example with the students. Ask them to locate the figures in positions B3 and D3 and to describe the figure between these two locations. (It has six equal sides.) This figure is drawn in the Example. After completing the exercises, verify that students have located and drawn the correct figures by asking them to verbally describe their solutions. Note that F–127 has two solutions.

ANSWERS:

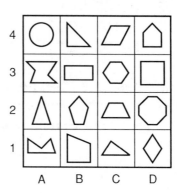

Draw the figures below that are in the following locations on the chart.

Example: Between B 3 and D 3	F–123 Between C 2 and A 2
F–124 Between D 2 and D 4	F–125 Between A 3 and A 1
F–126 Below B 2	F–127 Above B 2

PAGES 275–282   READING AND DRAWING LINE GRAPHS

Mathematical Concepts
- Rectangular coordinate system (letter-number)
- Given coordinates, locate points
- Describing patterns on a coordinate system
- Given a point, determine its coordinates
- Comparing geometric patterns to coordinate patterns
- Drawing paths on a coordinate system

VERBAL ANALYSIS STRATEGIES AND ANSWERS

❑   PAGE 275: This page introduces a series of activities using a rectangular coordinate system. The coordinate system uses letter-number coordinates to locate *points* where lines intersect. This differs from the previous activities which used coordinates to identify *regions*. As in previous activities, stress that the vertical (letter) coordinate is written first and the horizontal (number) coordinate second. Discuss the Example with the students. Ask them to locate the vertical line identified by the letter A (using their fingers or a colored pencil). Also, ask students to locate the hori-zontal line identi-fied by the number 2. Find the point where these lines intersect. (It is marked with an X.) Repeat this process with the other three coordinates. Ask students to describe the pattern formed by the four points marked with X's. (All points lie on an oblique straight line.) After completing the exercises, verify the solutions by having students describe each pattern formed.

ANSWERS:

Example:
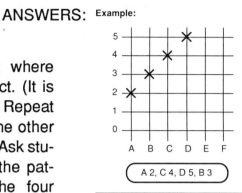
A 2, C 4, D 5, B 3

F–128
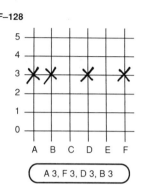
A 3, F 3, D 3, B 3

F–129
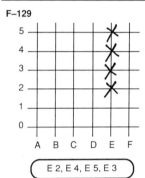
E 2, E 4, E 5, E 3

F–130
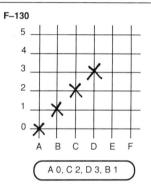
A 0, C 2, D 3, B 1

❑   PAGE 276: In this continuation of the exercises on page 275, remind students that the coordinates identify a point that is the intersection of two lines. After completing the exercises, have students verify their solutions by verbalizing the patterns formed. This can be done in many ways. For example, in F–132 the pattern could be described in one of the following ways: 1) the points lie on two oblique parallel lines, 2) they lie on three vertical parallel lines, or 3) if connected, they form a trapezoid.

ANSWERS:

F–131
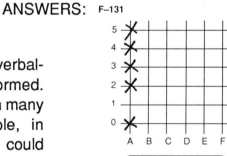
A 2, A 4, A 5, A 0, A 3

F–132
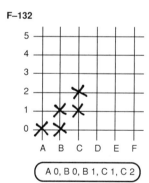
A 0, B 0, B 1, C 1, C 2

F–133
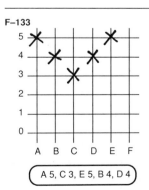
A 5, C 3, E 5, B 4, D 4

F–134
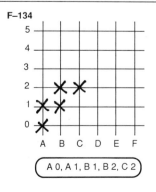
A 0, A 1, B 1, B 2, C 2

❑ PAGE 277: The tasks on pages 275–276 are reversed on this page. Points on the coordinate system are marked with X's and students are asked to write the coordinates of these points. Discuss the Example with the students. Ask them to locate the highest point marked with an X and name the vertical line through the point. (E) Name the horizontal line through the point. (4) What are the coordinates of this point? (E4) Stress that the letter is written first. Verify that this point (E4) is in the box, then repeat the same process for the other three points in the Example. Since students may not list their solutions in the same order, compare lists to verify solutions.

ANSWERS: **F–135** [B3, D1, E5, F0]   **F–137** [C4, D3, E2, F1]
              F–136 [A0, B1, D1, F1]

❑ PAGE 278: These exercises continue those from page 277. Have students verify solutions by comparing their lists. After completing the exercises, discuss the relationship between the patterns of points and patterns in the list of coordinates. For example, in F–138 the points lie on a vertical line through C and all the coordinates in the list begin with C. In F–140 the top two points lie on a horizontal line through 2 and the coordinates of these two points end in 2. Discuss other such relations between points and coordinates.

ANSWERS: **F–138** [C0, C2, C3, C4, C5]   **F–140** [A0, B0, B1, B2, C2]
              F–139 [A3, B3, C3, D3, E3]   **F–141** [B1, C2, D3, E2, F1]

❑ PAGE 279: Students are asked to write the coordinates of five points on a path drawn on a coordinate system. First students must locate the five points on the path where the grid lines intersect. Then they may proceed to write the coordinates of these points as before. Discuss the Example with the students and ask them to mark the five points on the path using X's. Two of these points are endpoints, two appear at square corners, and one is the midpoint of the horizontal line through 1. Now ask students to locate the coordinates of each of these points in the box below the Example. After completing the exercises, ask students to verify their solutions by comparing lists. Their lists may not be in the same order, but they must contain the same five coordinates.

ANSWERS: **F–142** [C2, D2, E2, E3, E4]   **F–144** [B0, C0, C1, B1, B2]
              F–143 [C4, C3, D3, D2, E2]

❑ PAGE 280: This page is a continuation of page 279. Again, ask students to verify their solutions by comparing lists.

ANSWERS: **F–145** [A0, B0, B1, C2, D3]   **F–147** [A0, B1, C2, D3, E4]
              F–146 [C3, D3, D2, E1, F1]   **F–148** [A0, B1, C0, D1, E0]

136   P.O. BOX 448, PACIFIC GROVE, CA 93950

❏　PAGE 281: The tasks from pages 279–280 are reversed here. Students are given a set of five coordinates and asked to locate the five corresponding points and connect them in the order they are listed. Discuss the Example with the students and ask them to locate the five points by placing an X on each point. Then ask the students to verify that the drawn path connects the five points in the order that is listed in the box. After completing the exercises, ask students to compare paths to verify that the points are connected in the correct order. If some paths do not match, one of two errors may have occurred: points may be located incorrectly, or the points were not connected in the order listed in the box.

ANSWERS:

Example:

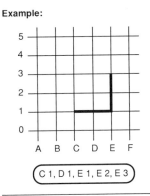

C 1, D 1, E 1, E 2, E 3

F–149

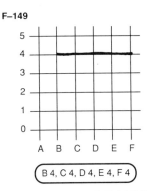

B 4, C 4, D 4, E 4, F 4

F–150

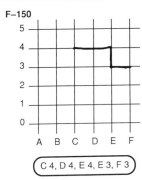

C 4, D 4, E 4, E 3, F 3

F–151

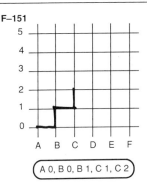

A 0, B 0, B 1, C 1, C 2

❏　PAGE 282: This page continues the activity from page 281. Have students verify their solutions by comparing paths. After completing the exercises, note that the path in F–155 forms a closed figure that is symmetric. The lines of symmetry are the vertical line through C and the horizontal line through 3. What two coordinates must be added in F–154 to make a closed figure that is symmetric and uses the vertical line through D as a line of symmetry? (E3 and D2.)

ANSWERS:

F–152

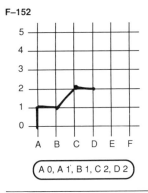

A 0, A 1', B 1, C 2, D 2

F–153

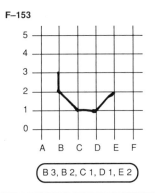

B 3, B 2, C 1, D 1, E 2

F–154

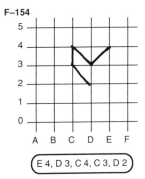

E 4, D 3, C 4, C 3, D 2

F–155

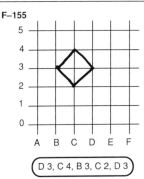

D 3, C 4, B 3, C 2, D 3

EXTENDING ACTIVITY MASTERS

The following activity masters are for use in the practice and extending activities suggested in the Number and Numeration, Geometry, and Measurement sections of this book.

NUMBER LINES

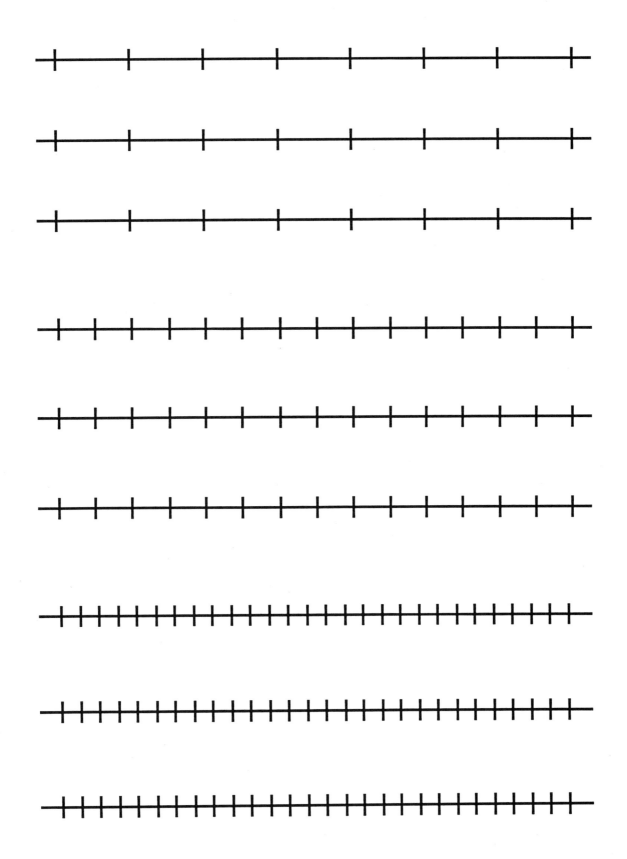

GEOBOARDS

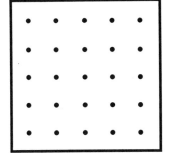
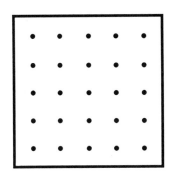
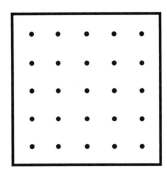

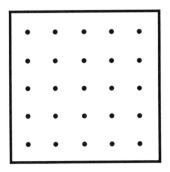
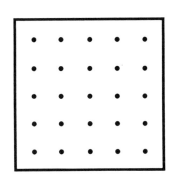
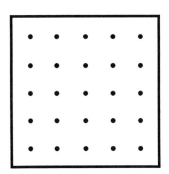

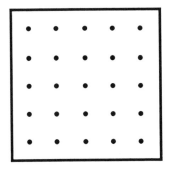
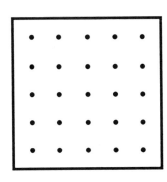
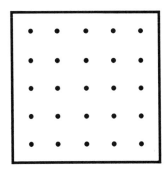

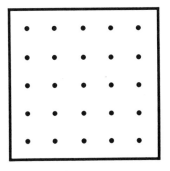
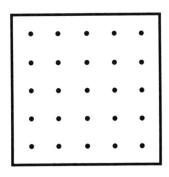
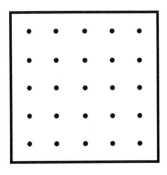

GRIDS

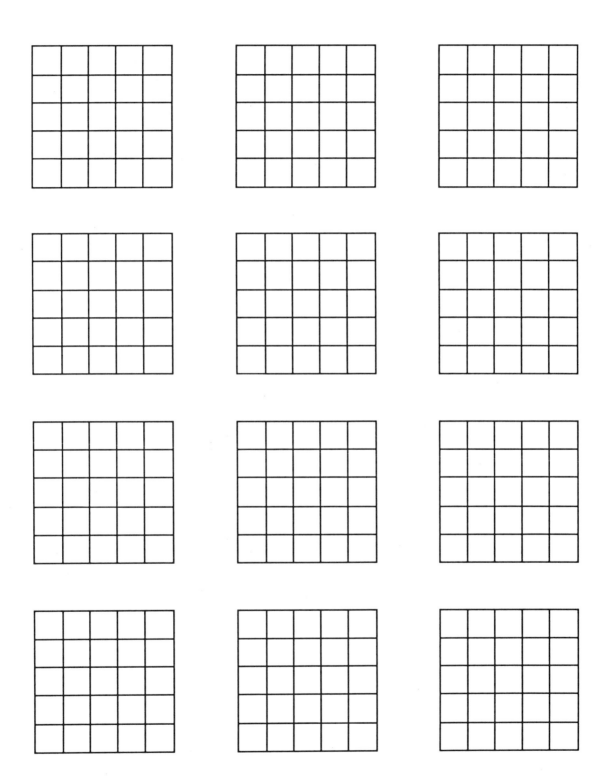